THE REASON

"A book with this much substance will, without a doubt, live on to change lives for generations. I truly believe Lacey's story has fallen into your hands at the perfect time. Dive right in and find out the reason."

—from the foreword by **Brian "Head" Welch**, lead guitar for Korn / Love & Death, author of *Save Me from Myself*

"Fresh. Passionate. Powerful. Lacey Sturm does in *The Reason* what she has done her whole career—she tells the truth, sings the truth, dances the truth. Her story will blow you away, and her heart will touch you. Read *The Reason*. Just like her voice and presence, Lacey's writing compels and penetrates, and in the end she will change you."

—**Chap Clark, PhD**, author of *Hurt 2.0: Inside the World of Today's Teenagers*

"In a time where the gulf between sacred and secular seems to grow incrementally, Lacey bridges the gap with her soul-bearing candor, raw passion, and prophetic insight. She communicates the comedy, tragedy, and triumph of her life story with fluidity and grace, and her message is timelessly impactful. It 'screams' of Jesus Christ, who is alive and active today, even in our darkest times, and the great news that no one is beyond his reach."

—**John L. Cooper**, lead singer of Skillet

"At its core Lacey's story is one of hope. From desperation to redemption to victory, this is an amazing journey that, apart from God, would not be possible. Hers is a story that will encourage and challenge all who read it."

—**Michael W. Smith**, singer and songwriter

"I have been fortunate to witness Lacey grow from singer/ songwriter to wife to mommy to now author. She is an amazing soul with a heart like no other. Her life and her story have been such an encouragement to me, and I know this book will also inspire and change you forever."

—**Sonny Sandoval**, lead singer of P.O.D.,
founding member of The Whosoevers

"Lacey has touched so many lives around the world through her music. Her story will hit your heart."

—**Ryan Ries**, cofounder of The Whosoevers

"Lacey Sturm is a voice of hope to a hurting generation. In her book, you will experience God's unstoppable heart for you and for those in your life who need a supernatural reset. Lacey's message is real, raw, and dripping with love. Dive in and be blessed!"

—**Nick Hall**, founder and primary
communicator of PULSE

THE REASON

how I discovered a life worth living

Lacey Sturm

BakerBooks

a division of Baker Publishing Group
Grand Rapids, Michigan

Published by Baker Books
a division of Baker Publishing Group
P.O. Box 6287, Grand Rapids, MI 49516-6287
www.bakerbooks.com

Printed in the United States of America

Library of Congress Cataloging-in-Publication Data is on file at the Library of Congress, Washington, DC.

ISBN 978-0-8010-1673-8

Unless otherwise indicated, Scripture quotations are from the *Holy Bible*, New Living Translation, copyright © 1996, 2004, 2007 by Tyndale House Foundation. Used
by permission of Tyndale House Publishers, Inc., Carol Stream, Illinois 60188. All
rights reserved.

Scripture labeled KJV is from the King James Version of the Bible.

To protect the privacy of those who have shared their stories with the author, some
details and names have been changed.

Ilustrations by Jordan Clarke, www.jordanclarkdesign.com.

Published in association with Yates & Yates, www.yates2.com.

14   15   16   17   18   19   20   7   6   5   4   3   2   1

To Brittany Wigand. Thank you for caring about the passerby behind the music you fell in love with. Your story always reminds me of how God can turn my worst moments into glory in the lives of others, if only I will let him. It's with you—your encouragement and your story—in mind that I wrote this book. I believe in you so much.

To the one like my teenage self, who is a breath away from finding the beauty of a life worth living.

To whoever needs to know that God loves you and has a plan for your life, and though you will die one day, he doesn't want you to die tonight.

You are important, loved, and prayed for.
Love, Lacey

Contents

It would seem that our Lord finds our desires not too strong, but too weak. We are half-hearted creatures, fooling about with drink and sex and ambition when infinite joy is offered us, like an ignorant child who wants to go on making mud pies in a slum because he cannot imagine what is meant by the offer of a holiday at the sea. We are far too easily pleased.

C. S. Lewis, *The Weight of Glory*

Foreword

*T*here is a state of being that, unfortunately, countless
people have fallen into. A place so empty that words fail
to accurately express the hopelessness felt in the soul. The
person feels completely and utterly lost. Besides the heartbeat
keeping the body alive, all else seems dead.

The end.

But that very "end" can become a new beginning where
a brand-new structure rises out of the gloom of emptiness.

There have been countless stories about this mind-boggling
change of existence, and my life happens to be one of them. I
cofounded the rock band KoRn in the early 1990s. My success
exceeded way beyond what I ever could have hoped for. But
my failures totally shattered all of my accomplishments, and
I was left to waste away in a prison of drug addiction, depression, and despair.

I was spared for a *reason*.

The heart of a human being isn't only an organ that pumps blood through the veins. The heart is at the very core of who a person is.

It has the capacity to experience the bliss of heaven.

It has the capacity to feel the miserable hollowness of hell.

Lacey Sturm has experienced both of these extremes, and she has been given an incredibly important platform to help turn our generation around.

I've known Lacey for a few years now, and her story will always be one of the most jaw-dropping life transformations I've ever heard. Each time I hear her story I can feel her hopeless pain and sorrow as she reached the point where she gave up on life after trying to satisfy herself with the world's antidotes, which only left her soul in agony.

Lacey was spared for a *reason*.

Pain is an interesting experience we all have to go through. In this race of life, pain has the power to drag us down and ruin the rest of our lives—or it can be used as wind under our wings to lift us to the glorious heights of destiny. We've seen it countless times.

Parents of a murdered child fall into a lifetime of depression—or they start an organization in their child's name to help others.

A rape victim becomes an alcoholic to deal with her pain— or she starts a program to help other rape victims get past the horrors of their experience.

Lacey has yielded to the process of pain turned into power. She has lifted and inspired so many people, male and female, and this girl is barely getting started! Lacey is a true poet and songwriter who speaks the language of the heart. Her soul is a hope magnet for countless other souls slipping away into nothingness like she once was. I am proud to call Lacey and her husband, Josh, my friends, and I can't wait to see the results of this book for decades to come. A book with this much substance will, without a doubt, live on to change lives for generations.

I truly believe Lacey's story has fallen into your hands at the perfect time. Dive right in and find out the reason.

Brian "Head" Welch
(Korn / Love & Death)

This Today

I wasn't supposed to wake up today.

My bedroom here feels huge compared to the other places I've lived. It feels too big for a girl like me. Maybe one day I'll move into an old van and feel more at home. Over there is the poster of my dream car, a Volkswagen camper, hanging alone on the big wall across from my bed. An empty Ben and Jerry's chocolate chip cookie dough ice cream container filled with dried flowers sits on my dresser. It's from my "friend date" with Jacob. At the time, I secretly hoped he would break up with his girlfriend of three years, the one he fought with all the time, and fall in love with me. That way we could stay up late together, reading Robert Jordan epic fantasy novels.

Memory boxes fill the underside of my bedside table. One is filled with the evidence of my first love, Ryan—notes he gave me in between classes, the lighter I used to burn a smiley tattoo into my hand the first time we got high together, his copy of *The Vampire Lestat*, the book he was reading the first time I saw him, the one that distinguished him from the other seventh grade boys.

I have a drawer full of pictures that my little brother and sisters drew for me. They remind me to see the beauty in every day, to keep going.

A bass guitar sits in the corner wearing a fuzzy purple strap called Purple Haze. My backpack beside my closet door is filled with books and a script for a play I planned to audition for next Friday. I had tacked my ticket to next month's Pantera show at the Mississippi Gulf Coast Coliseum to the wall beside my bed, next to a picture of Dimebag Darrell I had torn out of *Guitar World* magazine.

This is how they would have found my room.

Apparently I had some dreams, goals, things I valued about my life. But if I'm honest, none of the things I thought mattered were really important to me. If they were, then I don't suppose I would have planned to kill myself yesterday.

But now, here I am. I'm here waking up. I'm rising to a new today. And this today looks and smells different to me. I'm just lying on my bed looking around, noticing all my stuff. But it feels like I'm really opening my eyes for the first time. On *this* today I forgot to hate that I woke up again, like I have done every morning for years. Something lingers in this room. It's something real and full of meaning.

What will replace my hate? Is it this lingering thing I feel all around me?

Today I'm fully alive—for the first time. And I don't want this freedom from my hate to go away. I want it to stay. I want it to soar. And I want to soar with it.

From
Shadows

Shadows remain. Daily we war with our own hearts, pushing down the hurt, pain, disillusionment, disappointment, bitterness, and betrayal. God's brilliance, however, compels us through the shadows. We long for it.

Timothy Willard, *Home Behind the Sun*

1

THE REASON
I Lived

*M*y mother lay unconscious, covered in blood. Blood smeared her face and hair and soaked her entire gown. Granny screamed for help.

The nurse rushed in and tried to calm her. "I know it looks bad right now, but she's going to be okay."

Eventually the nurse admitted that they had almost lost both of us, but they were relieved to stabilize my mother. They continued working on me, trying to help me breathe properly. But the whole scene was a mess, and this bothered my granny. And when Granny's bothered, you know it.

She cussed the nurse out.

"Why didn't you clean her off? Someone get some water and towels and clean the blood off my baby! I'm serious! Who treats people like this? I'm reporting this whole hospital! Get my baby something to clean her off!"

The nurse tried to calm her again.

"We've stabilized the mother, but we need to care-flight the baby to Miami, and we need someone to go with her."

Granny pointed to my sixteen-year-old mother and yelled at the nurse, "THAT IS MY baby!"

Now she began to cuss the whole hospital out.

"How in the world do you treat people as badly as this and still have a job here? I thought y'all were supposed to be helping people. She looks like y'all have been trying to kill her! How come nobody has even wiped the blood off her face and her little hands? I ain't leaving her with y'all! Look at her! No one is taking care of her!"

That was my granny: a striking twenty-nine-year-old woman with long platinum blonde hair that fell in beautiful heaps down her back. Her dark lashes curled long and elegant against her brows and revealed her deep blue eyes. Her penetrating gaze held steady and true, even when she laughed. Beautiful and unafraid, she had a passion for her loved ones.

My mother is her firstborn daughter. Still today, she calls my mom her baby. We are all her "babies" in her mind. Back then my granny would stand in a room wearing baggy sweats and drinking a Coke, saying nothing, just minding her own business—and capture a room with her beauty. That's the strange thing about physical beauty. It makes people notice, wonder, and doubt themselves. It can be a lonely gift.

As a child I looked at my grandmother the way a young girl would look at a real live princess. I hung on her every word. When she said my name or looked in my direction, I blushed and felt honored. When she praised me, I felt like everything was right in the world. She taught us to fight for what we believed in, to do whatever we could to help rescue whomever needed rescuing. She taught us to treat strangers this way, not just our loved ones. She raised one passionate man and three passionate women. Even at sixteen, my mother was passionate enough to risk her life delivering me, a child expected to die anyway.

And as my mother fought for me to live, not thinking of herself, Granny now fought for my mother, knowing that no one in that hospital loved my mom like she did.

It was suggested months earlier that my mother not risk having another baby. They didn't think it would be safe because of complications she'd endured while delivering my brother Eric just ten months earlier. Not only were there medical risks for both of us but it was also complicated because of what she had been through with my father.

He was a young, handsome Native American man. My mother said he was daring, protective, and had the most beautiful heart. But that was only when he was sober. The Hulk-ish person he became after a typical night of drinking landed him in jail many times. By the time my mother was pregnant with me, an extended stay in prison was just around the corner for my father. In the future, his stay in correctional facilities would bring him salvation in a few different ways, but at this point in time it only left my mother on her own, at sixteen, with one child and another on the way. So the doctors suggested she abort me.

My mother ignored their suggestion.

My granny continued to argue with the nurse until finally they sent me on to the hospital in Miami alone. My mother laughs now and says, "You were on tour from day one." Before I left for Miami, the doctors didn't hold out much hope. I was born two months premature, and since lungs are the last thing to develop, I was having some critical issues. They feared I would die at any moment because I couldn't breathe correctly.

Three days later, however, those same doubting doctors declared me a miracle. No one could explain why—no explanation, no real reason. I was breathing fine and could go home.

When they finally handed me to my mother, I was small enough to fit in the palm of her hand. She said I looked like a little monkey because I was covered in hair. I was so fragile she was scared to hold me, let alone allow anyone else to. She was afraid I'd break. Maybe this was why she was always so tough on me. Maybe she wanted to teach me to be much stronger and more unbreakable than I looked.

More to Overcome

Not long after I went home with my mother, I caught whooping cough. I once again struggled to breathe. I wouldn't take a bottle. I began to lose weight.

My mom took me to the emergency room, where doctors and nurses worked to bring me back to health. Eventually they wanted to transfer me to another hospital in a different town. My mother became distraught at this suggestion.

My mom had been trying to work things out with my dad. She was in love with him. She wanted him to be around to know his children. When my granny announced that she and her husband were moving a state away, my mother resolved to stay put with my father. She clung to the vain hope that perhaps having two children would curb his appetite for alcohol and violence. But now, with her mother gone and her love in jail again, she was all on her own.

Putting me in a different hospital a town away for who knows how long now presented more stress than just worrying if I was ever going to get better.

"But, what about my eleven-month-old son I have at home? I don't know anyone in that town. Where will we stay?" she asked.

The people at the hospital couldn't give my mother any answers for that. After asking around she finally found some friends who were willing to help out. It was a difficult thing to leave her son for an indefinite amount of time, knowing she would be so far away from him. But it wasn't nearly as difficult as what would come next.

We stayed so long in the hospital that my mother lost her apartment. Now she had two children and no home. I was getting better but had to be force-fed with a feeding tube. It can be fatal to force-feed a baby if the tube accidentally goes into the lungs instead of the stomach, and that can happen easily. My mother understood the risks, and felt uncomfortable trying to do it exactly right on her own. She knew it was an important part of my survival. So, with a heavy heart, my mom agreed to place me in foster care. There was a kind couple who were willing to take me home and give me the special care I needed. But by the time she went to pick up my brother, she had no place to live with him. It was hard to find someone willing to take both her and her son in until she could get on her feet again. She went over the desperate situation with some of her friends, and they gave her some logical advice.

"Listen, maybe you just need to think about making sure your son has a stable place to stay. There are lots of loving families who can't have kids that would take care of Eric with joy. It might be the best thing for both of you if you took him down to the foster care offices and let them try to find a good place for him." This was actually very loving and good advice. It was sensible. My mother did not want to give up her son. She had just given up her daughter! It was all too much. But she didn't know what else to do. Overwhelmed, she reluctantly agreed.

Her friends took her to drop off her only son. But that night, she couldn't sleep. All night long she wrestled with her decision. In the morning she was back in the foster care offices pleading with anyone who would listen.

"Look, I made a mistake. I shouldn't have left my babies. They need to be with their momma."

"Well, find a job and a place to live," she was told. "Keep your residence for three months, and we'll give your children back to you."

Eventually she met the requirements and got Eric back, but they wanted to wait until I was able to eat on my own. Finally, I was fat enough and well enough. Though my foster parents offered to adopt me, my momma, the state, and God decided she would be the one to raise me.

Cause and Effect

I survived, like we all do, against the odds. I should be dead. I should be a statistic. I shouldn't be scribbling all over this page trying to describe the indescribable. So what happened? Was it chance, an accident, or dumb fate that I'm here now, a thirtysomething rock-and-roll mom looking back and collecting pieces of hope to give you?

I don't believe in fate or accidents. I believe in cause and effect. Behind everything lies a cause, a reason. Why does the

26

sun rise? Because the earth revolves once every twenty-four hours. Why do we read? Because, some say, we don't want to feel alone. Why am I alive, writing to you? Because I want to tell you that miracles happen. Because I want you to know how precious life can be. Because I want you to know how valuable you really are. Because the world will throw lies at you—lies aimed at your heart, aimed to kill. I choose not to listen to those lies anymore. Cause and effect.

> You and I, we sparkle with reason, a cause, a plan.

Imagine the scene I described above—the blood, the profanity, the risk to give birth to a child all the smart people thought should be aborted. Now place it all in the hands of a God who cares and has a plan for each person. In the chaos, God's plan was working. His plan for me touched other people—they saw me live and not die; they saw the miracle.

Our lives stretch out like shafts of light reaching into the lives of everyone else. You and I, we sparkle with reason, a cause, a plan. We're like a giant web of light and meaning and sadness and wonder.

What if you and I lived like we knew this?

What if we lived with the confidence that comes from walking in the bright of day?

What if we treated one another with the love we desire for ourselves?

What would happen if we understood how our lives touch every person we encounter in this world?

I strive to rest in the fact that I am made for a purpose. Knowing my life has purpose gives me confidence. When I live in the light of that confidence, it can empower you—it can make you confident as well. It can help you see yourself in truth and live unafraid, and when we live unafraid we live in the light of love. For true love casts out fear. That's how we sparkle; that's the web of light I see stretching from heaven into my life, into yours.

Chances are, if we lived like we knew this, our lives would shatter much of the sadness and pain that are so common in our broken world. I like that thought.

> Death has to wait because I have a song to sing and so do you.

I entered this life barely breathing. But now I'm singing my song out loud, and I'm shouting the lovely sounds of life and grace and hope. I almost died, but death has to wait because I have a song to sing and so do you. My song sounds like the healing of a soul and the rising of life. What does yours sound like?

I'm no longer just barely breathing. I'm living in the cause and effect of a life seized. I have reason to breathe. Before I disappear into the sound, I want you to know The Reason.

2

THE REASON
I Love Jazz

*M*y mother is an artist. She writes her own music, plays guitar, and sings. And she loves jazz music.

I was five when my little sister was born. My mother named her Jazilyn, Jazz for short. I remember fighting in the backseat with my siblings, each of us yelling for my mom to intervene with justice on our behalf. My mother's response was to turn the radio to smooth jazz. She turned it up so loud none of us could hear anything else.

She played jazz in the morning as a way to get us up for school. I hated it. I hated it even worse when I would walk home from school with my friends and we could hear Kenny G's saxophone blaring from the open windows of our house. This meant my mother was in the living room, in spandex, doing her own form of yoga stretches.

I couldn't help but hate jazz music, since my mom loved it, and a big part of my life at that time was all about hating whatever my mom liked. Although I'm still not the biggest Kenny G fan, I've learned to appreciate and love certain types of jazz. I think jazz represents my family history well. It's my mother's life soundtrack. I've come to find both her and jazz music fascinating and inspiring, especially after becoming a mom myself.

Chronically Distracted

Jazz music makes a good soundtrack for a life of being chronically distracted—forgetting the past, living in the present, going with whatever you feel no matter what anyone thinks about it. Jazz is a genre of music that is distinguished because it is a constant flow of thought that has no pattern; it doesn't follow rules, it changes with the wind in a way, and you never can tell where it will go and what it will do. Like the time my mother was waiting in line at a restaurant and a woman walked in wearing strong perfume.

My sister, sensing my mother's disapproval of the scent by the way she was holding her nose and gagging, implored my mother, "Mom, please don't say anything." The woman did not correlate my mother's very loud gagging with her stinky perfume, so my mother helped her understand. "Excuse me? Uh, excuse me!"

Now the lady began to notice my mother.

"Yes, you. Uh . . ." Cough, cough. "Your perfume is making me nauseated."

Gagging and more gagging.

The lady looked at my mom, amazed, and said, "Uh . . . I'm . . . sorry?"

My mom took this to mean, "What can I do to help your nausea?" So she told her, "Could you please go somewhere else . . . like, way over there, please?" Cough, cough, gag, gag.

Jazz music breaks all the rules on purpose. Like when the Mary Kay lady showed up at our house. During her demonstration she was bewildered almost to the point of leaving as my mom ignored her instructions and put a pretty color of eye shadow on her lips.

"That is eye shadow, ma'am."

My mom just continued applying it.

"I know," she said.

I liked my mom's choice of eye shadow as a lipstick better than any of the legitimate choices of lipstick the Mary Kay lady offered. I thought to myself, *This is how the world gets changed. Someone says, "This is the way it should be, no matter what they say." And they turn out to be right.*

Jazz makes its own unpredictable, mind-blowing sense of whatever notes it decides to put together, and jazz keeps going long after you think it should have given up.

My mother is a living jazz piece. If you're expecting any other more predictable genre of music out of her life, she'll rub you the wrong way. But if you expect the unexpected, then maybe you can move along, laugh, cry, scream, and dance with the song of my mother.

I used to watch, fascinated, as she'd dress for work in the evening. She'd blow-dry her hair upside down and allow gravity to work its magic on it, getting it as big as possible. Then she would take a comb and tease the roots, making it even bigger. She'd blow-dry the sides out into two wings. Big silver hoop earrings dangled from her lobes and covered her cheeks.

I watched her apply her makeup with awe. Her eye shadow faded into every color of the rainbow as it spread from the corner of her hazel eyes all the way to her temples. Her lips gleamed with a shimmering shade of fuchsia. She wore designer shirts called "Wind Blown Duck" with a studded belt hanging on her hips. Her black leggings, splattered with different shades of gray, came just above her graceful ankles. Her pearl-colored toenails hid inside her pink snakeskin patent-leather high heels. She always completed the ensemble with her pink leather jacket. I loved the way the jacket smelled, mysterious and enchanting. It was the smell of a beautiful woman. It was the smell of a woman who understood what it meant to live in the now.

People don't know what to do with a person like my mom. How do you respond to a person who wears every ounce of her passion on her sleeve? But whenever I think about the times when things were hard, I remind myself that we struggled through together and made it together because of the artistry of my mom's life.

> That is the genius of my mom — full of the jazz that paints a different world.

I've come to love that about jazz music. I've learned to love that about my mom. We would be on our way somewhere in the car and suddenly she'd say, "Hey! I have the guitar; let's go to the botanical gardens instead." I love how she'd color with me and give Ken and Barbie an amazing pink, orange, red, and purple sunset on the wall behind them. I love how even if we could have afforded it, we still would never have bought greeting cards for anyone. Instead, we always made our own with poems we wrote and pictures we drew. That is the genius of my mom—full of the jazz that paints a different world.

Better Means Less

Mom taught us the importance of kindness and compassion. Being considerate of others was her chief value. We always put ourselves last. One time I came home and my older brother's bed was gone.

"Where's your bed?" I asked him.

"Mom gave it to Lilly and her kids."

"Oh." I thought for a second and then asked, "Well, what are you gonna sleep on then?"

"A pallet, I guess. I don't care," he answered.

I'd watch my mom give away our food stamps. I'd ask, "But Mom, what about our groceries?"

"God will feed us, Lacey," she'd answer, annoyed that I was questioning her about it.

She was always right. Several times she woke us in the middle of the night, before we were old enough to stay by ourselves, and piled us in the car to go help a friend who was having problems with her boyfriend, or whose car had broken down, or who needed a place to sleep.

"You never know when you will be in the same position. We all need help sometimes," she would say.

And she was right. I met so many generous people through-out my childhood who opened their homes to us when we had nowhere else to go, like the large Hispanic family of at least twelve people who all lived together in a tiny apartment. At night the bedrooms and living room furniture were all full of sleeping family members. During the day the kitchen was always filled with people cooking, cleaning, or preparing for the next meal. No matter how many people ate from the pot of beans and rice, it never seemed to go empty. When our family needed help, this family was an example of selfless generosity to us. They took us in, fed us, and gave us a space to sleep on their floor.

Another woman who loved us like we were her own family was a beautiful lady named Maureen. While my mother was going to school and working on music projects, Maureen picked us up from school and made us hot meals. When we stayed the night she made pallets in front of the TV, where we watched movies and ate popcorn. Popcorn still reminds me of the loving hospitality she showed us.

She often noticed when I seemed heartbroken, and she'd always ask me about it. This was a time when bullying at school was the most intense for me, so we talked about that a lot. She told me the story of the ugly duckling and said, "Lacey, you are so beautiful, but sometimes it's hard for others to see past the outside, or to see potential for the future. But one day, you will be a lovely swan, and everyone will notice your beauty! But because you were once thought to be an ugly duckling, you will be able to see the beauty in others that the world thinks unlovely. And you will be the one telling them they are beautiful, the way I am telling you. I know, because I was an ugly duckling too."

I read later on that "God places the lonely in families" (Ps. 68:6). Oftentimes I watched this play out for us when we struggled. My mother humbly accepted help whenever she felt she could trust the people offering it. There was an organization in my hometown called Mission Arlington. They would help us by giving us groceries sometimes, and make sure we had a nice Christmas. That's one of the reasons why I believed in Santa for so long.

But Better Is Hard

Sometimes the only food we had left to eat was the free lunch they gave us at school. But there were mornings when our family of seven hadn't eaten through the whole loaf of Mission Arlington bread yet (like we seemed to be able to in just one round of peanut butter and jelly sandwiches). So my mother would hand my brother and me a piece of that stale bread to eat on the way to school. Gross—I hated dry bread in the morning. I was always a little dehydrated when I woke up, and my mouth was always so dry that eating that bread by itself made me nauseated. I never wanted to eat it. I used to shove it into my mouth as quickly as I could so I could get it over with, knowing I would get in trouble if I didn't eat it. Once I caught my brother folding his piece up into a tiny ball, hiding it from my mom until he walked into school, and throwing it into the trash. After I saw that, I did the same.

But even though I couldn't stomach the dry bread as a child, I can stomach dry bread now. I don't mean the kind you eat. I mean the kind of dry bread that comes from sacrifice. I'm so used to that taste in my mouth that life feels empty when I'm not snacking on the dry bread of sacrifice. My mom built that into my siblings and me through her crazy jazz life. Her perspective, so odd and beautiful, gave me kaleidoscope eyes—sometimes all I see are those Barbie and Ken sunsets, only translated into deep hues of thanksgiving and contentment.

I can see now how overwhelming it must have been for her children to reject the only food she had to give them. I remember a road trip where my mom had spent the last of her money on some food for us. She bought me some Vienna sausages. I hated them immediately and didn't want to eat them.

"Eat them anyway," Mom said.

I tried. Again and again I tried. Then I began to gag. Then I started to cry quietly. My brother Eric mimed for me to hold my nose and eat it. So I tried doing that. It helped me get one down. But on the next one I breathed out a little, caught the taste, and vomited all over the car, my brother, and myself.

I can clearly see my nineteen-year-old mother's desperation at having the only money and food she had left to feed her child wasted. And like many parents who live stressed out over money and the situation their kids must endure, she snapped. She stopped the car and grabbed whatever she could of me—which was mostly my hair. She yanked me out of the car and gave me one of her most memorable "whoopings" right there on the side of the road.

Some lessons in life hurt. And it's easy to hold on to the hurt. Bitterness always lurks in the lingering hurt. Being hurt growing up is real, even if it's for a good cause. I know helping others was great, but I didn't always understand how sacrifice worked. It hurt, and it seemed to lead to more hurt and tension. I'm not a teenage single mom with multiple children I can barely afford to feed, and yet I still have my own meltdowns as a mother. I can't imagine what it would be like to have been in my mother's position on that day.

As I look back now, I can see that grace is what we lived on.

God took supernatural care of our family. I didn't understand the concept of grace until much later in my life, but as I look back now, I can see that grace is what we lived on. Worldly logic would tell you that we should have ended up lost, dead, in jail, and eternally wounded by bitterness. But there was always a mystical protective grace over us.

I believe it was the grace of God that always covered the struggles we endured. Now this thirtysomething woman looks back on that dry-mouthed little girl and smiles and cries and sees how bitterness works, how hurt builds and stacks like bricks into a prison. But struggling through to survive doesn't come with an instant joy guarantee. It comes with nothing, really.

And sometimes that's what it feels like—fighting just for your family to survive. But with time, these stories have unfolded into something glorious. I believe God turned our struggles into something full and beautiful, like jazz. Our lives weaved in and out, surrounded by harmonic overtones and glimmering with the pain of my mom doing the best she knew how with what she had.

In the mornings I don't scrounge around looking for bread to give to my family. But I do scrounge around looking for ways to paint our life together with the kaleidoscope lens of a life lived like jazz. How am I doing, Mom? Can I borrow your pink leather jacket?

3

I Became an Atheist

I was ten years old. I was supposed to be asleep on Gramps's itchy brown tweed couch, but the TV was on. I can never sleep when the TV is on. The house was dark and everyone had long since gone to bed. So it was just Pat Robertson on the *700 Club* show and me.

Pat was showing videos about starving children in Somalia. There was a toll-free number on the bottom of the screen to call if you wanted to obey Jesus and donate money to these widows and orphans. If you didn't know Jesus as your Savior, you could call the number to pray with someone and become his follower. I kept looking at the phone on the end table above my head. My heart was burning in me to help these children somehow, but I didn't have any money. So instead I called and prayed with someone to become a follower

39

of Jesus who, Pat said, was a God who loves kids and cares about widows and orphans.

That same year I became an atheist.

Kelton—we called him Kelly for short—was our cousin and my little brother Phillip's best friend in 1991. They were both three years old. Kelly and Phil were obsessed with the Teenage Mutant Ninja Turtles. They had the same spiky mullets with cool steps shaved on the sides of their heads and wore multicolored and puffy MC Hammer pants with elastic around the ankles. Each of them wore awful smelling cowboy boots. Quite the get-up. They were hilarious and too smart for three-year-olds.

One time my Aunt Tera, Kelly's mom, was driving around doing her errands while Kelly and Phil sat in the backseat. Aunt Tera told us that suddenly she realized how quiet they were back there. When she glanced in the rearview mirror to check on them, she saw two three-year-old boys wearing nothing but their stinky cowboy boots.

It turns out they both thought it would be fun to take off articles of clothing and hold each piece in the roaring wind outside the window until the wind snatched it away. Over and over they let each piece of their clothes fly out the window until they wore nothing but their beloved boots. All Aunt Tera could do was to drive the naked boys home and clothe them again.

A Turning Point

Mrs. Woods was my teacher that year, in fifth grade. I was sitting in her history class learning about Paul Revere's role in the American Revolution. It's weird how you remember those kinds of details when an experience changes your life. My stepdad at the time showed up at Mrs. Woods's classroom door with a note excusing me from school. On the way to the car I asked him several times why we were getting out early.

Nothing, not a word.

We got into the car and waited. I remember the silence. Finally, I saw my brother Eric walk out of the school building and head for the car. That's when I realized something might be wrong. When Eric climbed in beside me we hounded our stepdad until he finally told us.

"Your cousin Kelly is dead."

At that moment I hated my stepdad worse than I had ever hated anyone in my life. He was the kind of guy who joked too much. He was always making up weird lies to shock us, just because he thought it was funny. I did not believe him for a second, and I hated him for saying something so sick and horrible. I slumped down in the backseat and stared with hatred at his big ears poking out from behind the headrest while he drove. I wanted so badly to just punch him in those big ears.

I hated him all the way home. Until I saw my mom.

This was the first time I remember seeing my mother really cry. That was when I knew my stepdad wasn't making up a sick joke. He was telling the truth.

But even then I didn't get it, because I didn't really understand what it meant to be dead. I remember sitting on a hotel bed in Houston, Texas, listening to the news in the background. I listened to see if they mentioned my cousin at all, since up to that point no one had wanted to tell me the truth about what happened to him. *Surely they'd mention a three-year-old child dying on the news*, I thought.

Although I never heard them mention Kelly, there were many stories of children being killed somehow. The news anchor talked about the horror stories like she was giving an uneventful weather report. She made it seem like children died all the time in Houston. It made me think the city had to be the worst city on the planet. My aunt had recently moved here from Arlington, where she'd lived for a year next to us in the Arlington Oaks Condominiums. I thought Houston must be a dangerous place for kids and wanted to get out as soon as the funeral was over.

The hotel room was packed with my relatives. My brother Phillip was sitting next to me on the bed, and I could tell my Granny was lying by the way she stumbled to say her words in an extra-sweet voice.

"What happened to Kelly?" Phillip asked her.

"His daddy was playing with him and . . . and he just played too rough. He hit him in the stomach too hard . . . on accident and . . . and now Kelly is with Jesus."

At the funeral everyone went up and kissed the body. Looking back, I think having a child kiss a dead body is a terrible thing to do. But I don't think any of us really knew what to do. It was like my little brother was in that casket. He was such a special little person to our family. Everything was so unexpected.

Boyz II Men's version of "It's So Hard to Say Goodbye to Yesterday" was playing while the line of people made their way from the casket to my aunt to hug and kiss her. When it was my turn, Eric Clapton's "Tears in Heaven" was playing. Today it's still hard to hear that song. When I saw Kelly, he was wearing his Ninja Turtles shoes, and some of his toys lay in the casket with him. *How strange*, I thought, *toys in a casket.*

But the strangest thing was the idea of my cousin being buried. When I saw him at first, I remember thinking, *I knew it wasn't true. Kelton is right here!*

I don't remember who was with me, but they told me to kiss Kelly when I approached the casket. When I did, it was like I'd kissed the sidewalk in the winter. That was when I knew what it meant to be dead. My cousin Kelly was not there. I think I must have repeated that phrase in my head in that moment while I looked at his frozen face.

My cousin Kelly is not here.

That was not him in the casket. It was a shell that looked like him. That's all. Time stopped in that moment. I bent a little on the inside that day. I think I grew up in a slightly crooked way from that instant on.

I didn't see people or bodies in the same way. A strange coldness settled over my heart. I now possessed a vague sense of the fragility of life. But more than anything, I had a deep sadness that wouldn't lift for the next six years.

> It was like I'd kissed the sidewalk in the winter. That was when I knew what it meant to be dead.

When I looked closer at Kelly's little body, with scattered bruises everywhere, it made me think about what my granny had said.

My mom didn't lie to me though.

She told me right away that Kelly was beaten to death. My mother never lies to make you feel better. I think she thinks it's healthier to face life as it is and deal with it the best you can—at the very least *realistically*. She viewed sheltered people as naïve and easily duped. She loved her children by making sure they would not grow up naïve.

I Stop Believing in God

That was the moment I began to question God. He was supposed to be good. I thought he was supposed to be *so* big. Kelly was so very small. His stepdaddy was so tall and bulged with muscles. How could God let something like that happen to someone so small? God was supposed to love children, right?

I was with my aunt when she returned to get some of Kelly's things from their apartment. She picked up his Teenage Mutant Ninja Turtles pillow and hugged it so tight. She buried her head in the pillow and inhaled, closing her eyes. "It still smells like him," she said.

The saddest thing to me in that moment was that she didn't have her husband to hug her. He was in prison forever now, for murder. And I had heard scattered conversation about how he may not live that long in there because people in prison don't treat child abusers or child killers with any kindness or mercy.

> I thought I had to be the best god I could be, because if there was a God— which I doubted— he was obviously not going to help us.

Even though they had terrible fights, I knew my aunt had loved her husband. How could God let all this happen to her? She was my hero. She loved me when I felt like I was just in the way all the time at home. I wanted to be just like her. I think it was in the room where Aunt Tera hugged Kelly's pillow that I stopped believing in God.

I wanted to hug that pillow so bad, but I didn't want to take any of the smell away from Kelly's momma. That was all she had left of her only baby. This was the beginning of an emotional imbalance in me, one I continue to struggle with. It's this constant tug-of-war that I have to be a protector, deliverer, and savior for all those around me. I thought I had to be the best god I could be, because if there was a God—which I doubted—he was obviously not going to help us.

It was impossible for me to believe in God at this point because I knew that if there was a God, he *must* have made people for more than just dying horrible deaths, more than going to prison, more than the deep depression I was sinking into.

But maybe God hadn't made us for great things after all, I thought. *But who cares anyway?* I didn't believe in God anymore, and that was that.

How Doubt Leads Us to Light

When Kelly died, I felt a part of me die with him—my belief in anything good, in anything beautiful, in anything having to do with this so-called God. Pat Robertson had said that Jesus loved children. But because of death itself I decided to stop believing that. Death didn't just happen to bad guys, like kid movies seemed to teach me, and death didn't just happen to old people who had lived full, happy lives, like I'd thought. Death was a huge, dark, scary mountain to me as a child. This mountain of death shot up from the ground, and I was suddenly lost in the middle of it. I felt like I was left to find my way out all alone. What I didn't realize at the time is that love is stronger than death. I wouldn't know love until it was almost too late.

4

THE REASON
I Fell in Love with Sadness

*W*hen I returned to school, things didn't feel right. School was so bright and colorful. There was laughter and joking, games and music. It felt wrong for me to be going to school and moving on with life after the death of my cousin. When recess came, I wandered around the playground thinking about him. Then I saw his name. Totally amazed, I stood and gazed at the "Kelly" printed on the side of one of the tires that led up to the jungle gym. I climbed up onto the tire and ran my hands across the letters. I spent the rest of recess sitting there thinking of him, wanting to tell him I was sorry that everyone seemed to expect me to just move on with life.

After recess came music class. The music teacher handed us the lyrics to the song she was about to teach us. When I saw what the song was, I felt all the blood rush to my face. My heart started racing. It was the same song that had played as I waited in line to view Kelly's body. I tried to figure out if this was supposed to comfort me or if it was supposed to spark a meltdown. I stood and watched nervously as the teacher started the song. Did I want to hear it? I felt like I had to decide right then what my response should be, all on my own, all in the small time span between receiving the paper and the beginning of the song.

> I chose to love Kelly by being sad. I was going to try to remember to be sad always.

It wasn't enough time. I was overwhelmed with a desire to honor my cousin somehow. I wanted to respond to his death—the right way, the loving way. I guess I just needed to mourn, but at ten years old I didn't really know how.

"Okay, class, I want you to read along with me as I recite the lyrics."

She began. Something told me to be angry, to run away, to not stop hurting. Something told me this was meant to hurt me over and over and that it would never stop.

"The song is called 'It's So Hard to Say Goodbye to Yesterday.' It's by a group called Boyz II Men," she continued.

As she recited the lyrics, my heart wrenched with uncertainty. The familiar words spoke about longing for the past, but also about losing a future. It expressed the pain of having no more tomorrows with your loved one. Someone told me recently that one of the hardest parts of a divorce, or loss of a job, or when a child passes away, is the death of a vision. And I experienced that firsthand as the teacher read this first part of the song.

She had not finished reading the whole song before I made my decision: I would mourn. I chose to love Kelly by being sad. I was going to try to remember to be sad always. In this small way, I was saying to him, "I won't move on without you. It isn't fair. And though I'm not dying with you outwardly, I'll at least stay close to death inwardly."

After she read the last words of the second chorus, I shot up from my chair and ran out of the classroom. I couldn't listen to the song. I wouldn't listen unless I was alone and could relive Kelly's funeral and weep. It felt like the only loving response to my ten-year-old heart. After I slammed the door open I ran to hide on the playground. I went straight to the tire with Kelly's name on it, climbed up on top of it, curled up in a ball, and cried.

I cried because I was sad but also because I was angry. I was angry at the world for telling me to move on. I was angry at the school for being colorful and jovial. I was mad at people for being happy, for not mourning with me. I was angry that people all around me went about their business as usual as if we didn't live in a world where children got beaten to death.

Whenever the world around me was happy, it felt deceitful. It all felt fake and foolish and ignorant—on purpose. It made me angry at everyone. It made me want to hate them all. I was mad at the Texas sky for being sunny that September day. It felt inappropriate. I felt like the whole world was in on this deception—like even the weather was smiling at me and telling me to move on already. But I wasn't falling for it.

Instead, I fell for a worse deception—one that would try to steal my life along with my cousin's. The deception I was falling for looked much more honest in those moments. Life was all wrong, and I could throw it away if I wanted to. It may be honest, and it may be half true, but it is not the whole truth, and therefore, it is a lie—a lie meant to kill me within the next six years.

If only I had stayed for the ending of that song, where the vocals soar with hope and purpose without compromising the honesty.

Toward the end of the song the voices remind the listener of memories. If you move on through the rain, the lyrics suggest, sunshine will be there after a while. They encourage you to find ways to make the life of your loved one count. By letting the good memories of their life make your life more colorful and bright, you will, in turn, illuminate the lives of those around you. In this way, even though it's hard to fathom while it's raining, while you are mourning, while you can barely bring yourself to say goodbye, the sunshine will come. You just need to keep going.

> If only I had stayed for the ending of that song, where the vocals soar with hope and purpose without compromising the honesty.

If only I had been teachable and let the lyrics remind me that there were beautiful memories to hang on to. There was an amazing little life that had been a gift to the world and to our family for three years. If I kept on living, then my good memories would live with me, and then my memories and I could, perhaps, in some small way, make the world better somehow. There may actually be good that could come after the bad.

There was the possibility that prison for Kelly's stepdad actually saved my Aunt Tera's life. That man had come close to killing her during one of their bad fights. If only I would have known that it was okay to mourn—that sometimes rain can be overwhelming, but that doesn't mean that the rain will never stop. And that sunshine after the rain makes rainbows visible. Thunderstorms can be signs of spring. If only I had seen that there were good memories to focus on and not forget. Maybe then I wouldn't have chosen to start down that dark, reckless, hateful, lonely path toward death.

Learning Abuse

The year Kelly died was also the year they started teaching us about abuse in school. There were four different kinds: physical, sexual, verbal, and emotional. Some of the videos I saw looked pretty similar to stuff that happened at my house. Before watching those videos I didn't know what abuse was. Though the videos helped me understand what abuse was, they really didn't help my family or me at all.

After watching those videos, whenever I was hit or yelled at, I would go to my room and write it all down in a journal. Suddenly I felt like a crime had been committed against me. I would cry to myself about how my mom didn't love me. This new information about abuse just made me feel sorry for myself to the point of depression and self-loathing.

This was the beginning of the years I would cry myself to sleep.

Although it seemed like a gradual process, the videos that classified some of my mother's actions toward her kids as abusive, when all she was trying to do was raise us the best she knew how, really shut down my ability to be positively affected by her by the time I was in the sixth grade. I unrealistically expected things to happen in a certain normal way because of those videos. When they didn't happen that way—because "normal" was never a category my family fit into—it caused an unprecedented sadness and self-pity that took control of my heart. It made me emotionally unhealthy.

Seeing those videos at school when I was ten was a major turning point for me. I became addicted, at a very young age, to feeling sad and sorry for myself. I think most people would call this depression.

I thought about suicide all the time.

There were five of us kids at that point. My mom wanted us to go to a nice school and live in a better neighborhood than we could afford. So we all lived in a one-bedroom efficiency condominium in a place called Arlington Oaks. There were two mattresses on the floor in the living room. One for the boys, one for the girls, and then my mom and our youngest baby sister, Stevie, slept in the bedroom. We ate on a pink plastic tablecloth we rolled out onto the floor by the kitchen.

The humid Texas heat is the perfect environment for roaches. And we had them in our condo as well. There were definitely times when we all felt crowded in such a small place with six people and the unwelcome bug families. The tension of our circumstances added fodder to the reasons I found to be sad in those days. My sadness could fill every square inch of the air in that place at times. But there were also two toddlers and a little baby who didn't yet know how to wallow in self-pity. For Jazilyn and Phillip, the situation intensified their ability and need to be creative in their playtime. It was their joy and gratitude that consistently interrupted my plans to stay sad.

Many times, because of the children, what had felt cramped all of a sudden felt cozy and magical. At night all of us kids would pile into the same bed. In the dark, there were no walls, no roaches, no messes. We could have been in a palace. Or in Neverland. But our favorite place to pretend to go was Disney World. Our voices would whisper back and forth during a game of storytelling. One of us would start and then each of us would add on to the story until our heroes, villains, and talking animals had died and come back to life several times.

For years, these magical moments weren't the ones that stood out in my memory. The thing I could remember best was the depravity of the sad moments. Those were the moments I was looking for, in a confused and twisted way. I didn't realize that I was doing this; I just thought I was trying to stay realistic and to not be naïve. I wasn't aware that I was teaching myself to use my mind to steal my own joy.

> I wasn't aware that I was teaching myself to use my mind to steal my own joy.

We did go to a good school, which only meant that the rich kids would bully us and make fun of our thrift-store clothes. This forced us to band together with the minority group of kids who dressed similar to us. These were the kids who had the same kind of stress we did at home. They were the ones who needed friends more than anyone. Sometimes I would get to visit my friends' homes, where I would discover that their imaginations were just as big as ours.

But many times I would find an affinity for sadness, darkness, self-pity, harshness, and coldness in these homes as well. This made me more comfortable. I related to the sad feelings in other people's homes because it felt familiar to what I swam around in most of the time in our cramped condo.

My mom kept us at the condo and in that school so she could finish art school and get a better job. She attended the Art Institute of Dallas to become an audio and video engineer.

An Orphaned Feeling of Unbelief

My mother has never stopped believing in God. The miracle of that, after everything she has seen and been through, is enough to make you question your own atheism. Because I was a rebellious teenager, however, the fact that my mother believed was all the more reason for me *not* to. One night, after an intense session of family fighting, my brother Eric and I ran out of the house. My mother screamed from the front porch after us, "You had better ask God to forgive you!"

My brother stood in the middle of the street and cussed the idea of God. I felt nervous for him because it was a moment of despair I hadn't seen in him before, but it resonated with me. I understood the orphaned feeling of unbelief. I understood the resentment of a heart that felt disregarded and mistreated by life.

My brother, my mother, and I were all meant for more than intense family fights. We may very well have been abusive in the way we all treated each other. To me, the saddest part about this is that our minds weren't made to think hateful thoughts.

> And now, dear brothers and sisters, one final thing. Fix your thoughts on what is true, and honorable, and right, and pure, and lovely, and admirable. Think about things that are excellent and worthy of praise. (Phil. 4:8 NLT)

Hateful thinking is not what our God-given ability to reflect and meditate is meant for. It is meant to be used to meditate on love, God, truth, beauty, honor—anything good. Our mouths weren't made to speak hateful words. They were made to encourage, to teach, and to speak truth in love.

We were not created so we could use our actions and words in an abusive way toward one another. God intended our actions and words to be used for loving one another. God did not intend for his creation to be abused by others—or to wallow in self-pity. God created us so that we could love both others and ourselves. We were not meant to feel abandoned. God made us so that we could experience his embrace and the embrace of others—he made us for a special kind of relationship, a covenant relationship. We weren't made for the kind of despair we lived in. We were made to live with hope, faith, and love.

Kurt Cobain pointed out that there is a comfort in being sad. It's dark and hauntingly true, at least when you're a young girl looking for something to cling to. Crying myself to sleep began to feel familiar, like a kind of home. Darkness can feel honest, and honesty can be beautiful and feel so inspiring. But darkness stops short of resolution. It's deceptive. You can't see all that lurks within darkness. The things that inhabit darkness live there because you can't see them; that way they can deceive you, pervert you, and ultimately destroy you from the inside out.

For so long I lived in the deceptive perversity of the dark. But when I was in the dark, I could *feel*. The feelings that come from darkness can be intense, like a roller coaster or a horror movie. We can easily become addicted to those poisonous feelings. But eventually they make us numb.

Humans are resilient, and we learn to cope with unhealthy pain by eventually becoming numb to it. Once we are numb to our addiction, it's hard for us to even feel alive without its "comfort." This deception is like a parachute with a star-shaped hole in it. The manufacturer has told us that his parachute is like none other because the hole in the top is extra large so we can see the stars on the way down. We buy into the pitch and end up being made to feel most alive by the things that will kill us.

> Darkness can feel honest, and honesty can be beautiful and feel so inspiring. But darkness stops short of resolution. It's deceptive.

The deception is evil in the sense that if we don't stop it, it will kill us. Sadly, we can even be aware that something is killing us, and yet ignore our self-preservation reflexes until all we have left inside us is a death wish. Our addiction is so exhilarating that we think we don't care if it kills us. We can't even imagine life without it. And when we do, we think it will be a worthless, boring life that isn't worth living. We get this warped idea because once the high wears off, we feel ragged, miserable, ugly, worn out, and tired.

So, even in those low moments, we still don't care if we die. We go searching for those familiar feelings again, this time fully acknowledging our own death wish. Strangely, we don't really know what death means. Our souls writhe, exhausted from our unhealthy addictions.

We may desire to sleep forever, *to rest*. But we have no proof that the rest we are longing for is what we will get when we die. I know a girl named Marlene who shot herself in the face. As she began to die, she sunk into what she calls a deeper despair than the one she was trying to get away from. When she was brought back to life, she knew that she could not get the rest she longed for through suicide.

> We have no proof that the rest we are longing for is what we will get when we die.

So we stagger toward death with reckless laughter or deep, sad aching, and as we free fall we tell ourselves this falling sensation means we are alive. But the leap we took to get that feeling is a leap to our own destruction.

The question then becomes, *What can save us and give us what we are restless for?* Not the world we live in and are rebelling against. That world can't fool us. And not the death we're plunging toward, the one we know nothing about. We just need the God who started life itself to tell us. If only he would rend the heavens and come down.

5

THE REASON
I Loved Nirvana

I was rich. The room was my own. Sure, the random alley cats my mom was always rescuing had claimed the space under my bed as their favorite pee spot, but everything else in the room was mine. And yeah, so what if I lived with daily sinus pressure headaches and could barely breathe in there because of my cat allergy? I had a room. I could close the door, turn on the boombox I got for Christmas, and pretend I was one of Janet Jackson's backup dancers while she sang about racial reconciliation and ignoring nasty boys. This smelly room was an eleven-year-old girl's refuge.

Our name had finally come up on the government-housing list. After looking at the available homes, we found our castle on Ida. Ida was a small street in the ghetto of Arlington, Texas. Our house was just four doors down from a local band called the Giant Dogs. The Giant Dogs made us all proud by naming their first album *Starving on Ida*. But I didn't become a true fan of their honest rock music until later that year. Up until then I had this understanding that music was for entertainment, and musicians were entertainers. So I only used music as a way to entertain myself. I would make up dance moves to pop songs with cool beats. The lyrics were more about rhyme and rhythm than anything else. I certainly didn't know what I was saying when I performed every word to Salt 'n' Pepa's "Shoop" for my shocked daycare worker. And I thought when the panel of teachers for the fifth-grade talent show had their jaws hanging open while a friend of mine and I sang the graphic lyrics to Janet Jackson's "That's the Way Love Goes," it was because they thought we were just awesome singers. I don't think the sexually explicit content was simply over our heads. I think we caught on to the fact that this music was meant for entertainment, so we took it that way. It was only a catchy beat.

But that year, in one night, all of my shallow feelings about music changed. My mom bought tickets for a concert in Deep Ellum and she took my brother Eric. When he came back that night he was mad because Mom had made him leave before the band trashed the stage. But he was surprised that she let him buy a tape. He said Mom liked the band because the singer stopped the show to yell at the audience.

"If I see one more guy grab and grope another girl, you're all gonna listen to feedback for the next two hours!"

He had my mother's respect after that.

She also liked the naked baby on the front cover of the tape she bought him. She thought that was sweet. My mother loves babies. Eric showed it to me. It was Nirvana's *Nevermind*.

I was disappointed that there weren't any lyrics to read in the booklet. Maybe he was singing about how crappy men can be to women. I was a little interested in who the singer was after Eric's little story. Why did he care about guys groping girls? Why was he willing to stop his show to protest them doing it? Maybe the point of him making music was more than entertainment? Why? The more I thought about it, the more I was intrigued.

I looked at the picture of the band inside and was shocked to see they were dressed like us, with stringy, dirty hair. Eric had to use my room to play the tape since I had the only boombox with a tape deck in the house. I listened to it and was amazed. There was a hurt in the singer's voice, an aching that I felt in my heart and had never heard expressed in music. The music sounded like the way I felt when I cried myself to sleep at night.

At the same time there was this lightheartedness about the inner pain. It was kind of laughing at reality, but at the same time acknowledging the aching that comes with it. I could not stop listening to the tape.

Eric's birthday came up not long after that and someone got him Nirvana's *In Utero* on CD. I immediately devoured it. We had to play it in the big front room that my three little siblings shared because that's where the only CD player was.

Me, in Utero

I remember listening to the CD straight through four times, right away, going over the lyrics booklet as I listened, looking at all the details of the artwork, trying to see what it all meant and what it was saying about the band. They seemed like such a mystery, with their unintelligible, cryptic lyrics.

The lyrics seemed to say nothing solid and yet the screaming was so passionate. It *had* to mean something. So I just kept searching each time I listened to it. My favorite song off the album was "Dumb." It talked about being different from the people around you, getting high, and sniffing glue.

While I was listening through the CD the fourth time, night was creeping into the living room. I was sitting in front of the stereo, ten feet from the wall. On the other side of that wall was my mother's broken-down car. It sat on jack stands at the top of the driveway. "Heart Shaped Box" had just ended when the front of the car came crashing through the wall. CRASH!

It stopped just short of me.

I just stared at the rubble, so stunned that I couldn't move from the shock of what just happened. There was a car *in* the house!

Maureen, a close friend of the family, accidentally hit the accelerator instead of the brake when she was trying to park her car in the driveway and knocked my mom's car off the jacks, sending it into the house. That little incident etched *In Utero* into my brain—chaos, mystery, nonchalance, and randomness all happening in the music, in the room with the car crashing through the wall, in my life. Indelible.

The Uncool Becomes Cool

The year after I found Nirvana, Kurt Cobain committed suicide. When I heard it on the news, my eyes filled with tears. *Now I'll never get to marry him*, cried my unreasonable twelve-year-old heart. But his death also somehow made me more committed to Nirvana. Suddenly Nirvana was a legacy to be honored, and Kurt's suicide seemed heroic to me in some way.

Kurt seemed to think being famous and thinking you're better than everyone was so very wrong. Even at twelve, I understood the disdain for fame and the hatred of pride. I thought his suicide was courageous.

The saddest thing about my hero's death was I didn't realize it was wrong. I didn't realize that life—all life—possessed a magical kind of value.

Looking back, I can still find so much truth in Nirvana and what they stood for. Kurt's suicide, however, makes me sad.

When you're twelve and you already have it in for society and fame and all of what makes pop culture churn and the money pour in, you look to those who dare to be individuals as the epitome of life, even in death. Somehow Kurt's death felt like life to me, as twisted as that sounds.

Why did it feel like life to me? All the stress and weirdness I experienced in my life had a lot of darkness that came with it. And then something happened: I found a way to turn all the bad and dark into my identity. It felt honest and real. I felt comforted in finding someone who was suspicious of all things fake and of ignorant bliss. I was empowered in my suspicions by a public voice like Nirvana's that called out what everyone was being fed as the trash that it was. But I didn't know that you don't have to be suicidal to be brave enough to call society's bluff, and you don't have to be eternally sad to rebel against it.

> I didn't know that you don't have to be suicidal to be brave enough to call society's bluff, and you don't have to be eternally sad to rebel against it.

It was like I was standing at a crossroads where I could see only two choices: either I could embrace all my pain and *become* it, or I could try to be one of those shiny happy people I didn't trust. Wasn't their situation a choice for them? Maybe their seemingly fake happiness was exactly what my sadness was—a way to cope with all the garbage of life.

My friend told me once that sometimes the sad place where we keep ourselves feels like free falling. It's exhilarating even if it's a fall into a dark place. I used to look at darkness and find it so deep and intriguing. I loved this about Kurt Cobain. He was honest. And being honest felt so much closer to being right. But eventually the shadows of darkness overwhelm and actually become part of you—that's what happened to me. It begins with rebelling against all the shiny happy people. Then it turns into a thirst for sadness. And it bends and twists into a very dark, animal-like thing, as if the sadness has given birth to an evil so sly and cunning that it seeps in and suddenly you're contemplating death, like I was. Or cutting. Or puking your food out all the time.

Don't Be Brave

A few years back I traveled with a disaster relief organization called Samaritan's Purse to some far-off places in Alaska. In these tiny villages, the natives are on their own. It broke my heart to find out that suicide is their number-one killer. One teenager told me, after the death of a friend, "I wish I was brave enough to do that." But this is an example of how people get suicide so backward. It is not brave to kill yourself when things are sad and difficult; it is brave to live anyway.

It is brave to find ways to lay down your life to serve the people around you.

It is brave to forgive and to choose to love those who hurt you even though they don't deserve it.

It is brave to trust that the God who gave you life in the first place has a good plan in mind, even when everything around you looks like hell. It is brave to live.

I recently met a brave man from Alaska named Bill, who grew up in the trenches of what many of the suicidal kids in these small communities deal with. One of his earliest memories as a child is his loud, obnoxious uncles prodding him to down tequila shots at just five years old while his father was passed out upstairs.

His parents divorced because of his father's drinking problem. His mother worked three jobs to support the family on her own and was rarely home. A close male friend of the family sexually abused Bill for several years of his childhood. When he reached his teen years, the man verbally and emotionally abused him, and threatened to kill him.

But I love the way Bill's story doesn't end there. Bill encountered Jesus and found deep inner healing from everything he went through. Bill was brave enough to *live*, even after all the pain he endured. And now he is the president of a wonderful suicide prevention program called Carry the Cure for native teens in his area.

Kurt Cobain could have led millions into a kind of life where fame didn't matter, where pride was replaced by serving your fellow man. But he got out. He left us all in the lurch, wondering what to do.

It's amazing to think of it now, because when I read about Jesus I can't help but come away with a feeling that, although he was superhuman, in many ways he was also as regular as Kurt Cobain, except Jesus chose death in order to give us all life—a life that means something, a reason to live.

The same day my mom's car came through the wall, there were some walls that came down in my heart as well. Walls that were meant to keep me safe. Walls that taught me that suicide was wrong. Walls that kept me from self-destruction. Nirvana's message of humility would soon become perverted into self-loathing. Their message of compassion and empathy would become perverted into depression and deep sadness over the darkness in the world. My newly understood identity was now becoming warped. I didn't realize I was made for more than self-hate, depression, and a future of suicide.

6

THE REASON
I Stopped Caring

*S*eventh grade is a whole new universe. It holds the world of junior high, the world of romantic feelings, the world of being forced to shed your childish identity and scramble to search for a new one. There is heat, pressure, chaos, and the setbacks of finding foolish ruts.

Attending a new school with strangers was nothing new to me. I was almost snuggling down in the comfort of being the girl no one knew or cared to know when I walked into Mrs. Mackelway's science class for the first time. There was one seat left in the corner behind the door when I slipped in just after the bell rang. It was the perfect seat, the kind most likely to help me blend into the wall. Blending into the wall was one of my main objectives in school. I didn't want to draw any more attention to myself than I had to because

I knew I was fair game for bullying. My height, physique, thrift-store clothes, nerdiness, and thick glasses, coupled with my gross feelings of being ugly and stupid, seemed to produce the perfect homing device for bullies. So I was happy to find a spot where no one noticed me.

But Mrs. Mackelway gave me a look that said, *I notice you. And I also notice that you're tardy*. It also indicated that she was going to let me slide, just this once. As she addressed the class, I slid my hand into my partially opened backpack and quietly removed my paperback copy of Anne Rice's *Interview with a Vampire*. I held the book under my desk as I pulled out the pen I was using as a bookmark. I then opened the novel to where I'd left off. But before I could situate myself to see the open pages in my lap, I heard Mrs. Mackelway change her tone.

"This is a science class, and it isn't very friendly toward vampires."

I looked up like she'd caught me. I was relieved to find she was looking in another direction. I followed her gaze to a boy who was leaning back in his chair, holding the sequel to the book I was reading, *The Vampire Lestat*, boldly in front of his face.

"Well, as a science teacher, you should know that blood is an extremely important part of biology, and I can assure you that vampires are very interested in blood," said the boy without putting his book down.

My stomach turned into a ball of knots at his impudence. This is the kind of behavior that warranted swift, angry discipline in my house. "You wanna be smart? Who do you think you're talking to?" my mother would yell as she stormed toward me demanding respect for her authority.

I was nervous to see how the teacher would respond.

Mrs. Mackelway smirked. I was amazed. Had this guy overruled her with his carefree attitude?

"Well, unfortunately for you and your argument, biology is currently a ninth grade course. I'm afraid you're going to have to put your vampire books away while you're in seventh grade physical science."

The boy didn't move as he finished the page he was on.

"Ryan Burris?" said Mrs. Mackelway, in a more authoritative tone.

"Oh, huh? Yeah, yeah. Touché, Mrs. Mackelway, touché."

He smiled at her with a look of victory on his face. His teeth were crooked. He wore braces but they hadn't fixed much yet. His big, proud, crooked smile seemed to be another way to flip off society's idea of perfection, and I found this to be absolutely beautiful. His dark brown hair fell just above his shoulders, long, straight, parted down the middle, and shaved underneath. The only things that had a brand on him were his well-worn Airwalks. His oversized blue flannel shirt looked like he could have gotten it from the same thrift store I got mine from. On the side of his shoe he had a small scribbled drawing of a marijuana leaf. I had almost the exact same drawing on the inner sole of my Converse All Stars.

Ryan was still leaning back in his chair when he tossed his book onto his desk and crossed his arms over his head. He flicked the pen in his hand the way someone would flick ashes off of a cigarette.

Ryan did not fear authority like I did. This intrigued me. He respected being taken seriously, even though he was being a total smart aleck. He liked Mrs. Mackelway for being willing to be a smart aleck back.

Ryan tucked his hair behind his ears and finally looked in my direction. Embarrassed, I quickly looked away, hoping he didn't notice how long I had been staring at him.

Stale Cigarettes and Cheap Deodorant

Every week Loretta's mom hosted a Bible study at her house. Loretta was my friend, so I went to hang and hear about Jesus. A group of us got high before we headed over to her house. Ryan came too.

We devoured her mom's freshly baked banana bread. Then we sat in the living room while Loretta's mom talked to us about God and Jesus and all of it. Although I felt welcomed and loved, I could never remember anything she said about him. After she finished talking, Ryan invited me into the backyard to have a cigarette with him.

"Did you finish the book I let you borrow yet?" he asked me as we walked around the side of the house.

"Almost," I answered as we sat down on the grass with our backs against the brick wall.

He lit my cigarette and took a drag before he handed it to me. The crickets seemed like they were making some passionate speeches about life being deeper than we knew it was.

I wasn't looking at him, but I could feel him staring at me. He wasn't going to stop until he had my full attention. I was so nervous I felt like I was going to throw up. Finally, I looked up to see that he was completely sure of himself, even a little intimidating. His mature eyes held me still while he spoke his mind.

"I'm not interested in dating a bunch of girls. If I'm gonna go out with a girl, I want something that's going to last."

I thought about the story he'd told me about his parents. They'd stayed together since high school. What a legacy. How romantic.

He looked at me like I was supposed to answer. I didn't really know what to say. But every movie I'd watched since I was little had taught me that it was time for me, as the girl, to make the move to kiss him. I hesitated, not sure if that was the right thing or not. When I finally made up my mind, the moment I went in to kiss him he turned his head and I landed the kiss on his cheek. He turned back to me with a surprised smile.

"Did you just try to kiss me on the lips?"

He was making fun of me now, the way he did to everyone. I was so embarrassed. He put his arm around me and pulled me closer to him. He smelled like stale cigarettes and cheap deodorant. I found it lovely. His smile got bigger, then giddy. I still wasn't sure whether he was making fun of me or not.

Then he kissed me.

I knew in that moment I was wanted. It was one of the first times in my life I felt *chosen* and *wanted*. It was the deepest emotional experience I'd ever felt.

Real Friends Don't Light Themselves on Fire

Ryan and I had been dating for two years. There seemed to be thousands of traumatic events that I managed to survive. One day we were skipping school and hanging out at my friend Adam's house. The party was pretty small, but I guess we felt like we were a pretty good group of friends. Until the day Mike Hall invented the phrase "You just pulled a Mike Hall."

He'd just bought a Zippo he was proud of. He kept flipping the top open, lighting it, and swiping his hand through the flame. I guess he got bored with that because he started lighting the fringe of his jeans so he could watch the flame run up his pants and burn out. Suddenly he was stomping around the room with his leg completely on fire. My friend Amy grabbed a pillow and smothered the flames. When she pulled the pillow off, all of the skin on his leg came with it. He was in a lot of pain. I felt awful for him.

"You're an idiot! What, do you have no brain at all? You could've burned my house down!" Adam yelled.

The profanities flew.

"Hey, stupid! What's wrong with you? You almost killed yourself and got us all busted!" yelled Ryan.

More and more profanity was spewed.

"We have to call someone to take him to the hospital," I protested.

"No! That stupid moron has to get out of my house now! He's got to go sober up so no one thinks we do idiotic crap like that here. Let him find his own ride to the hospital."

Adam and Ryan had no sympathy for the whimpering boy. He was a stupid idiot and that was that. They kicked Mike out and made him walk home.

> I used to think partying together was a legitimate way to connect with people. Suddenly I got a vague sense of just what a cheap façade it was.

That was the first time I had seen such a horrible thing among my group of "friends." I wondered for a split second what dumb party foul I would have to pull in order to get kicked out and left to walk home by myself with a serious injury.

It was my first taste of just how shallow and fake drug-centered relationships can be. I used to think partying together was a legitimate way to connect with people. Suddenly I got a vague sense of just what a cheap façade it was.

But when I looked at Ryan, he consoled me by urging me to laugh at Mike. It was supposed to make me feel like I was different from him. It was supposed to reassure me that Ryan didn't just use me because I was convenient, like he seemed to use Mike. I was on the inside of his heart and it was *us* against the stupid idiots. He loved me. We were each other's first love, and he was committed through thick and thin.

Right?

Christmas Break

I hadn't seen Ryan since I'd left two months earlier. Even though my mom had sent me to live with my grandparents a few states away, we both promised to stay together.

"I'll see you at Christmas," he said.

"What a perfect Christmas present," I said through tears as he kissed me goodbye.

He had cried too that day.

Christmas break had finally come. I told my mom I was staying the night at Loretta's. As soon as she dropped me off I called him.

"Surprise! I'm here. Come see me! I'm at Loretta's."

"You're here?" he said slowly.

"Yes!"

Pause.

"Lacey, I need to tell you something."

"What is it?" My heart sank as I recognized his bad-news voice. I hoped no one had died.

"You were gone so long, Lacey." He sounded like he was going to cry.

"What do you have to tell me?" Now I felt like crying, not sure what he would say.

"I slept with Alicia."

I was completely shocked. The phone dropped out of my hand and I didn't realize I had stopped breathing until Loretta asked me what was wrong. That's when I finally caught my breath enough to weep, to mourn.

When Ryan said he slept with Alicia, it was like he had said the name of dozens of people. I had art class with Alicia, and therefore was forced to overhear her loudly and proudly tell her detailed stories of who she'd slept with that week as we worked on our projects. It was always a different guy. She was disgustingly flippant about a subject I really wanted to believe could be sacred. I always felt relieved to have barely missed being the way she was, because I had met Ryan. I was so thankful for him. But I was naïve.

> I realized how someone could stop caring about sacredness, because in this moment sacredness felt deceitful.

Maybe Alicia already had her heart broken the way mine was now breaking. Maybe she was flippant about love because "love" had been flippant with her. Maybe she didn't care about love, because love had not cared about her. In this moment I realized how someone could stop caring about sacredness, because in this moment sacredness felt deceitful.

The sacredness of my relationship with Ryan poured beautiful promises out of our hearts and into each other. I believed with everything in me that we were so very different. Every other relationship out there in the world had nothing on our love. They didn't know us. They didn't understand us. They might fail, but we never would. We were perfect together. We were perfect.

That's how much certainty I had about our relationship. I believed everything we said to each other. All of our "forever" and "never" promises were true, at the time. Ryan taught me to stop caring about what people thought—authority figures, my friends, who cared what they said.

But on this day he taught me to stop caring about the sacredness of romance. If time can change a promise, no matter how well-intentioned or how heartfelt and meaningful, then all the promises we made were lies, right? From perfection to lies in the span of one short phone call.

I believed in Ryan the way I now believe in God: I worshiped him. But that is too much weight to place on someone you care about—too much for anyone. It turns out no one is god enough to be God except God himself. Ryan was just a sixteen-year-old boy who needed a savior just like I did. But in that moment, all I could do was mourn the death of my idolatrous relationship. I longed to die with it. I had one less reason to care about living.

I'm so thankful that my story does not end here. Romance, friendship, leadership, and love have turned out to be so much more than I ever thought they could be. All earthly versions of these things are merely dark reflections of heavenly ones. At the time I could not fathom there was something deeper and more real than the love I had felt with Ryan.

But the truth is, a true and perfect love does exist. It dives deeper and shows itself more real and reaches far beyond all we could ever imagine.

> But the truth is, a true and perfect love does exist.

And this kind of love is not confined to romantic sexuality. It is a love that makes up heaven itself. It is the kind of love that corrects but shows grace, that discerns yet defines total abandon, that seeks the truth even when the truth is not popular. One day soon I would discover this kind of love, on earth as it is in heaven.

7

THE REASON

I Wanted to Scream

I was stealing my brother Eric's weed. It was my justice for him pawning my CDs. I wasn't too worried about the Dinosaur Jr. album I got for my birthday, or the Cranberries record I was over, or even the Bush album, since I'd already memorized all the bass lines. As much as my brother made fun of me for it, it was the Beatles Anthology double disk my mom had bought for me. That's the one that made me want to get bold and flip him off right back. For my mom to buy me something like that when we had utilities being cut off was one of the many scattered moments that year when I felt my mom's love for me.

So even though stealing weed was normally taboo even in my own moral code, I felt like he deserved it. He couldn't tell on me (ha!), so it was even more of a crappy thing to do.

But he got me back. On this, my third time stealing from him, I went into the shed where we hid our paraphernalia and grabbed his lighter and his last little roach. With the lighter almost touching my lips, the flame shot out and burned the eyelashes off of my left eye. He had turned the flame from low to high. As much as I wanted to cuss, I had to laugh at the foresight he had to orchestrate such a perfect retaliation. I stormed into the house to congratulate him on being so smart.

I could hear his sorry excuse for a new favorite band, like a battering ram against my brain, blaring through his bedroom door. When I opened it, there he was flailing around his room, screaming mysterious, angry—and no doubt obscene—lyrics along with Phil Anselmo. I had to admire his complete disregard for my own disdain for this massacre to the human ear called Pantera.

"You know, this isn't *really* music!" I screamed over the noise.

He turned it down to show me the censored version of the cover of *Far Beyond Driven*.

"Does Mom know you have that?" I asked, immediately noticing the Parental Advisory logo.

He ignored my question.

"Pantera is local. Right here in Arlington, Texas," he said. "This guy literally lives around the corner from us."

Apparently our stepdad had gone to junior high with the guitarist, Dimebag, and his brother Vinnie.

"Guess what junior high they went to? Ours! All three of them went to Gunn Junior High in Arlington!"

I didn't believe him, thinking someone had just been trying to sell him a CD. But he was adamant.

"I'll prove it to you. I'll get an old yearbook from the school library."

Curious, I let him take me to the library the next day. I love anything to do with going back in time. When I actually saw the pictures of these guys in the 1981 yearbook I was intrigued. How could a band my stepdad was friends with, who were from our hometown and sounded like trash, make it so huge?

That day when I got home I picked up the CD booklet with the lyrics for *Far Beyond Driven* and began to play the songs, reading along with the lyrics. There was a lot of perversity, sacrilege, blasphemy, and godlessness that I felt was a bit unnecessary.

Even as an atheist I thought that kind of thing was just a tacky and slightly dishonest way of shocking people—until I got to a song called "Shedding Skin."

"Shedding Skin" explained all the screaming perfectly.

The screaming was really the thing that bothered me about Pantera. But it turns out there is no other honest way to sing such painful, angry lyrics. It was a story of horrible abuse. These lyrics, if sung honestly, must be screamed. It reminded me of stories I heard of boys being raped, something that made me want to scream and cuss and murder. And here it was being emotionally vomited in the most perfect sound to describe such a hate for such an evil. It was the sound that comes out of someone who has been scarred by that kind of abuse.

The song may not really be about sexually abused children, but when I thought about it for the duration of the five and a half minutes the song played, I felt a great shift in my heart. It was a *kairos* moment—a specific time in my life for specific action. It was the birth of a new sense of purpose, something I clung to desperately in those days of feeling like my life was just a burden to the world around me.

Someone had to scream about injustice.

Someone had to scream with passion.

Someone had to scream like Jesus did on the cross over the evil in the world.

I didn't believe in God at the time, so I opened my heart to the drunken rage of Phil Anselmo against his own demons.

Guided Screaming

I believe each person is created with passion. Sensible, respectable voices of the world do their best to dim our passion, because someone driven by passion could cause a cultural stir. Passionate people can be dangerous, reckless, and revolutionary, for better or for worse.

I saw many things in life that stirred me, that angered me, that confused me. I knew in my core that there was something very wrong with the world. I possessed a strong sense of its injustice, like it caused a fire to boil in the center of the earth, and everything was tainted by the smell of its sulfur rising from cracks in the earth's surface. Screaming was my natural response to injustice.

I knew in my core that there was something very wrong with the world.

I guess I've always searched for truth. Whenever someone was bold enough to scream about something, it made me think that person must really believe what he or she was saying. Like screaming was some kind of truth serum. I assumed whenever people screamed, their heart of hearts would be wrapped up in the loud voice somewhere. Many times when someone screamed at me, my reaction was either to receive what was being screamed as truth or scream back—my clarion call to right the injustice.

When I started writing music with screaming in it, the point was to hit someone back. Singing, speaking, yelling—it all felt like an appropriate response to being alive, like I had a responsibility to change the world because I was breathing, and so my voice was meant to be a tool of change. Before I believed in God, my venting, ranting, and screaming always had some searching in it, but most of all it felt like I possessed a destructive power over the things I hated. There was honesty in my hatred, and even back then, some of my hatred and anger were flung toward gross evils.

It felt good to think I had a voice in life, even if only I could hear it.

So in cursing evil, I had a vague sense of being able to change it. But my idea of justice against evil was, many times, just more evil in return. After God rescued me, however, I found a purpose for my screaming: to speak truth over the lies in people's hearts. Lies like the ones I believed about myself when I wanted to die. Lies like, "Joy will never come," or "Nothing can break the chains around my heart," or "Everything would be better if I wasn't alive."

Injustice exists in the world—like people using our God-given gift of speech to make others believe they're worthless. I used my voice as a judge, calling some people worthless. The ones who abused and used others were worthless to me, so I sang, screamed, spoke out about them. I screamed for anarchy because I witnessed abusive authority. Anarchy appeared to be justice for the abuse of authority. I screamed because it felt like something to live for. It felt good to think I had a voice in life, even if only I could hear it. It felt good to stir up passion over anything. It made me feel alive and gave me a vague sense that my life had some small impact or meaning.

Sometimes things will stick in your gut and drive you nearly insane when you think about their injustice. For me, it is atrocities like human trafficking, rape, sexual abuse, violence against defenseless victims, and so many other issues. God places these passions in our hearts so we will never forget the good, so we will never forget that someone always needs help. So many people live twisting in the wretched winds of despair and grief and anger, and they do so in relative silence. My passion, my drive, was to scream because it felt right. It felt like it might change something in some mystical way. It felt a little like prayers feel to me now: like my most honest response.

When I encountered God, I noticed that many Christians weren't passionate about much, at least on the outside. Maybe I was screaming because in some odd way it put me closer to a God *I know* cares about injustice—it breaks his heart. The broken heart that makes me scream comes from the broken heart of a God who moves within me, aching and yearning for his creation to know how beautiful, valuable, and loved it is.

Phil Anselmo helped me understand that there is something wrong in the world—an injustice to scream about, an injustice to try to remedy.

But God helped me understand that his heart breaks when we hurt. He helped me see his compassion and lovingkindness. He also revealed to me that he is a roaring lion of a Father who wants to end our brokenness. In fact, he became broken himself in order for us to become whole and healed and well.

Later, the Bible would also confirm that my words can be creative and also destructive, and that the passionate heart behind my words can and will change the world for better or worse. But God still trusted me with a voice. There would come a day when I would pray for him to use it to bring life to people who had been destroyed by other voices—lying voices. I prayed God would use my voice to scream justice over every lie seeking to destroy the very people he made for great things. That's all of us. If only we would believe that truth! If only we could reject every lie that tells us something different.

8

THE REASON
I Wanted to Die

*T*he first story in the Bible is all about the importance of words. The whole first chapter of Genesis repeats: "God spoke!" And it happened.

"God spoke!" And it happened.

"God spoke!" And it happened.

Then God makes a human, gives him breath from his own mouth, and tells him to speak. But I never needed the Bible to tell me how life and death lay in the power of the tongue. I could feel it for myself when certain people spoke to me.

"You're ugly."

"No one likes you."

"You're stupid."

"You're always in the way."

"I hate you."

I felt myself begin to die. Then God would send another voice along.

"You're beautiful."

"I like you."

"You're smart."

"You're a good helper."

"I love you."

Then I felt myself coming back to life.

I don't believe bullying is the main thing that makes us want to die. I believe that it can be a trigger for people like my young self who already feel unsure about their purpose and identity—people prone to sadness, people restless with a world that seems to offer so many shallow answers to the deep questions that make their hearts heavy.

But even though it isn't the only cause of people wanting to die, verbal and emotional abuse are powerful and destructive in the mind of someone searching for identity. For years I carried a heavy backpack full of destructive words. I learned to be clever and poetic in my hatefulness by pulling things out of my backpack that others had put in there. I learned the demonic "wisdom" of verbal and emotional abuse by being that demon's target.

I was also versed in the demonic "wisdom" of lying, cheating, stealing, manipulating, arguing, arrogance, gossip, division, and on and on. I kept building my arsenal in order to do things that I considered to be good. I found noble reasons to exercise these demonic "wisdoms." I convinced myself that as long as I was accomplishing a greater good in the world (whatever I decided good was), I was more than justified in using any of these weapons. And I was deeply offended by the concept of *sin*. I felt like it was just a vindictive tool for the people who wanted to point fingers at you, to make you feel like crap and control your life. So I purposely dove into what I knew to be a Christian's view of sin. Anytime I met someone who hadn't been "liberated" by enjoying these "sinful" things in life, I would work really hard to "set them free" by getting them to do the thing they considered most taboo.

Any moral compass I possessed was fueled by my emotions. I let my emotions dictate right and wrong to me. I called this "listening to my heart."

I let my emotions dictate right and wrong to me.

As I dove into my ever-changing morality, it all kept my heart distracted. And I had to stay distracted so I could keep telling myself that I was fine. But when everything got quiet and everyone went home, and I was alone in my room, I could sense emptiness growing inside me. Not being able to sleep was horrible, because when I laid on my bed at night, I felt myself opening up to a scary reality, a reality that whispered, *You're just fooling yourself, Lacey.*

Maybe I was just ignoring reality by being distracted. I felt restless and agonizingly uncomfortable with myself when I was alone. I felt sick, wrong, and messed up, but I had no language to explain it and no answers to understand why. Of course, most of the time I could see what hurt my body, and often I could see what would help me heal: time, a bandage, some Neosporin.

And I could see what hurt my mind. Most of the time I just needed to not get high before school if I wanted to do better on my first period math test. I could even see what hurt my emotions sometimes, and if I cared enough about a relationship, I could go to the person who hurt my heart, talk it out, and try to make it right. So even those hurts could heal.

But late at night, my restlessness, my strange, deep aching felt like it came from somewhere beyond my body, my mind, and even my emotions. There was this eerie nagging I didn't want to face that maybe there was more to me than

85

I understood; maybe there was something in my life I was hiding from. But to think that way forced me to face myself in a way I feared. It forced me to consider that I might be just as messed up as all the people I hated and thought were a waste of space, and maybe now I would have to face the same judgment I had cast on so many others.

When I'd reach the edge of myself like this, I'd start justifying all the things I was questioning in my heart. I would explain to myself why I was different, why I was justified, why I was excused. And eventually my thoughts would die down. My heart, mind, and body would feel exhausted. But something deeper in me still wouldn't let me sleep, and the restlessness, the aching, the empty feeling were still there.

And then, worn out on the inside, I'd begin to cry.

It was such a familiar feeling, crying at night. It felt like an appropriate response to life. Something just wasn't right about it, and there were no answers to make it right. There was a deep loneliness in those moments that I only felt in the mornings. The two quietest, emptiest, loneliest parts of my day were when I laid down and when I got up.

It's amazing to me that these two moments would soon be the most fulfilling times of my day. These moments would become the times when I felt the God I worked so hard to not believe in embrace me like no one else ever could.

Later on I discovered I'm not just a body with a mind and emotions, a heart and a soul. I would realize that within my soul there was a spirit that I was neglecting. Within my soul there was a spirit God formed to be the roots of all that I was. It would be my source of life—or if neglected or poisoned, my source of death. Even then I knew my body was more like my vehicle than my real self. But I only considered my self to extend to my soul: my mind, will, and emotions. So to find a deeper part of me was a surprise, a relief, and it

made so much sense out of so much chaos and
turmoil within me.

Pain made sense to me. I could feel it. It was
when I went numb to pain that I felt so anxious.
Eventually physical and emotional pain would
start to numb me completely. Bono
sang the truth I felt during this
time when he said, "The
only pain is to feel nothing
at all." It is one of the emptiest, deadest feelings.

You can see what hurts your body and emotions in this
life, but you can't always see what hurts your spirit. I think
my addiction to being sad culminated into an addiction to
rage and violence. I knew if I pushed my mother to a certain
point she would fight back. If my mom wasn't around, I
would push my older brother. If he wasn't around, it would
be directed toward people at school.

I loved to fight with anyone who was sensitive to being
challenged. I was so messed up that I would actually create
horrible situations in order to cry about the injustice of my
life. I would get bored with peace and act out, causing crazy
drama to ensue. *I was addicted to emotional pain.* If I didn't
have anything to hurt about in my own life, I would hurt about
something in someone else's life, like it was my own problem.

The emotional pain I desired deadened me.

Eventually life circumstances had to be traumatic in order
for me to be affected by them at all. But over time the pain
lost its flavor and I discovered I was numb.

Death and Truth

Though I felt numb, the insatiable desire for *something* still
existed in me. That never goes away. That's the very reason I

was in the place I was. I was seeking something beyond me, beyond you, beyond the gross pain in the world.

Writers of great literature talk about this deep desire. They call it *sehnsucht*, a German word that literally means "longing." A friend of mine showed me these lines from the haunting poem "The Buried Life" by the great poet Matthew Arnold:

> But often, in the world's most crowded streets,
> But often, in the din of strife,
> There rises an unspeakable desire.
> After the knowledge of our buried life;
> A thirst to spend our fire and restless force
> In tracking out our true, original course;
> A longing to inquire
> Into the mystery of this heart which beats
> So wild, so deep in us—to know
> Whence our lives come and where they go.[1]

I feel like I can almost reach out and touch the thoughts of this old poet. In these lines he describes the longing, the *sehnsucht*. One of my favorite writers, C. S. Lewis, also talks about this deep longing that propelled him toward an encounter with God. I didn't know it then but that deep desire, that desperate longing for something more, would also land me right in front of God, just like it did for Lewis. It's like that for us all, really. You and I experience a deep thirst for satisfaction. But this satisfaction does not come sexually, or through material possessions—though that is how we try to quench that desire. We think money will make us feel safe or content, but it only heightens the desire.

Lewis, or Jack as his friends called him, initially thought this deep longing was nothing more than romanticism. But

1. Matthew Arnold, *The Poems of Matthew Arnold* (London: Henry Frowde, 1906), 154–57.

through conversations with friends and his own reading of Christian authors, he realized that it was not a great poem or a beautiful song or a great book that would give him unending joy. Rather, it was the thing behind the poem or song or book—and that "thing" was God.

For me, though, this deep desire to be known, to be loved, to be healed, to be *satisfied* through and through drove me to places I never want to visit again, dark places. I'm not sure if Jack ever visited the dark places I frequented, but I'm sure he felt the letdown of thinking, *Aha! This will surely satisfy*, and finding that it was only a shadow.

Every morning I awoke feeling like a burden to the world around me. I wanted to disappear or find that *thing* to satisfy my deep desire. Let me say this about suicide: it's a liar. It will whisper to you and fill your mind with just the right amount of evil mixed with something resembling truth. But those are the best lies! Suicide will tell you to cling to the drama, to the people who hurt you, to the tough circumstances of your life and say, *Look at all this! It isn't worth it anymore. You aren't helping anyone. You make no good difference. You only make everything more inconvenient. You will always feel empty and achy. Living is too painful, so why are you doing it? You just need to sleep forever.*

> I didn't know it then but that deep desire, that desperate longing for something more, would also land me right in front of God.

The truth is that we do need rest, but not the kind that sleep gives. And believing that suicide and sleeping forever are the same thing is to believe a lie. Dead bodies only look like they are sleeping, and our bodies are only temporary vehicles anyway. Our vehicle may feel worn out, but our soul is the thing that needs help. And at a certain point the only help it can get is for the marrow of the soul, the spirit, to come to life.

We need rest for our souls.

My soul was trying to be its own life source because my spirit was so sick it was almost dead. And a soul trying to stay alive without a spirit is like a beautiful autumn leaf that falls from a tree. It may be beautiful and awe-inspiring because before it fell it turned the most intense red, and it may have looked exhilarating and alive even as it fell to the ground, but very soon that beautiful leaf will turn to dust. I thought that my soul was coming to life whenever I would listen to certain music, or read certain books, or find romance. But it never stayed. The brilliance of the colors would always fade.

I asked myself, *Do I long for something beyond the songs I love, beyond the books I love, beyond my boyfriend or girlfriend? None of that seems to really satisfy me. Is the answer to end the longing? Or is the solution to go into the beyond itself and see if the light has anything to say about what is dark?*

9

The Reason
I Couldn't Kill Myself

*W*hen Jazilyn came home from the hospital, I was five years old and officially a big sister. I took this position very seriously. I planned to teach her everything I knew. How to color, draw, read, make up stories, put on plays, make peanut butter sandwiches—everything.

She didn't start getting into trouble until she began to crawl. Boy was she fast! She always headed right for the cat food.

"No, no Jazz! That's Bowie's food! It's yucky for babies!"

"Thank you, Lacey, but I'm the momma. I'll take care of your sister," my mother would remind me.

Jazilyn was brilliant. She had white-blonde hair and big blue eyes. She looked like my granny. When she first started talking she would mimic everything she heard. She loved to pretend she was on the phone when you were and babble everything you said right after you said it. She was really good at sounding like whomever she was mimicking. We called her Lil' Mockingbird. By the time she was five she was an excellent impersonator and totally hilarious. She was a great performer and loved to put on a show. She is still one of my favorite storytellers. She and I have very different personalities though.

Jazilyn was definitely a girly girl. She loved to wear dresses and bows and wanted her hair fixed just so. She was organized and would collect all our junk mail and shove it into the ugly old purse we got her for a quarter at a garage sale. She called them her "important papers." She held that thing on her arm like it had gold bars in it. If you ever touched her purse she would start screaming like a banshee.

"Don't touch my important papers! Mooooooom!! Lacey is touching my important papers, Mom!"

When she ran out of room for the junk mail in her purse, she would put it in plastic shopping bags and carry that around on her arm along with her purse. Eric and I called her a "little old bag lady." That's what she looked like when we were walking through the grocery store with her wearing those ridiculous bags full of trash on her arm.

Phillip is a year and a half younger than Jazz. My little brother has always been a deep thinker. He feels deeply and had the most delightful mind as a child.

One evening all of us kids were sitting in the back of Gary's truck. He was my mom's good friend. He drove us along some country roads in the warm Texas night air. The sky was clear, lit up by a big bright moon. We all sang songs.

"Don't Worry, Be Happy."

"We Built This City on Rock and Roll."

"I Will Always Love You."

The stars shined brighter as the night grew darker. Eric led us all in the clapping song, "Deep in the Heart of Texas," to celebrate the glowing constellations above us.

I noticed Phillip wasn't singing or clapping. This was one of his favorites. He was staring at the sky, contemplating something.

"What's wrong?" I asked.

He looked at me with genuine wonder and concern and asked, "Why is the moon following me?"

I laughed. "Well, I don't know, Phil."

My Little Loves

The next day, Phillip had overheard my mom say something about how leather was stretched by getting it wet, so in the middle of his bath he ran and grabbed his almost-too-tight but beloved cowboy boots, put them on, and sat down cross-legged under the bubbles. When I went to lift him out of the water I noticed he was heavier than normal. The boots hung like buckets on his feet, gushing water all over me and the bathroom floor. After we all had a good laugh, I cleaned up the mess.

I was towel-drying his hair. He was watching himself in the mirror and admiring the new cool steps he had just gotten shaved into the sides of his head. Suddenly his face lit up.

93

"I know why the moon was following me! Because he likes my new haircut!"

"Of course!" I exclaimed, and congratulated him on figuring that out.

I was ten when Stephana was born. After that I lived for her smile. She was brilliant and enchanting. By the time she was three I had helped teach her to read and she could sing along with the Abbey Road CD I kept on repeat in my bedroom. One of her favorite movies was *The Lion King*. Every time the daddy lion would die she would run to me, climb onto my lap, and wrap her arms around my neck. Through her sobbing she consoled me, even though she was the one crying. "It's okay, Lacey. You don't have to be sad. He's gonna come back in the stars." She has always had deep compassion, grace, and a love for animals.

I was thirteen when Roman was born. My mom honored me by allowing me to be the one in the delivery room with her when he came into the world. I cried when I saw him. He was so magical and tiny. I wore a hospital scrub shirt, and I was the second one to hold him after my mom. The nurse put his little feet on an inkpad and lifted him up to stamp my shirt with his perfect little footprints. It was one of the most miraculous days of my life.

Roman was just as clever as my other siblings. More clever than me at times. Once, when I was making a pizza, I opened the oven door to check on it and flames shot out. The whole oven looked like it was on fire. I think I had forgotten to remove the cardboard from the bottom of the pizza. I stood there in complete shock with the oven door open.

Two-year-old Roman stood close by with his eyes bulging. My mind went completely blank, and then I heard myself say, "I don't know what to do!"

A little two-year-old voice behind me said, "Water! Get the water!"

Yes! I thought. *Getting water is what I should do.*

So I ran to the sink, filled a cup with water, ran back over, and tossed it on the burning pizza. We were saved! I turned around and snatched up Roman. My eyes filled up with tears as I thanked him and kissed him over and over.

"You are so smart, Roman! You saved us! I was panicked, but you knew exactly what to do! I love you so much!"

Living for Something More

I did love Roman so much. I loved them all so much. I thought through all these memories one night as I finished drying my hair. I lay down in my bed and let each one slowly talk me out of wanting to die. This was why I couldn't kill myself. I didn't want to hurt them.

I envisioned Jazilyn having to babysit the younger ones and how hard it would be on her when my mom was working. I didn't want to abandon them.

So my life was saved for a season.

But living *for* people will only last so long. One day my siblings would become more self-sufficient and would have other people in their lives to care for them better than I could. Then my reason for waking up wouldn't be there anymore. And then what?

> My reason for waking up wouldn't be there anymore. And then what?

Relationships, to me, are a big mirror reflecting the source of all relationships. You and I may love our families and our

95

significant others because we were created to do so. We exist on this earth as relational beings because we come from a relational God. He is Father, Son, and Holy Spirit—a community of beings. Some say we were created out of this loving community in order to create our own loving communities. So no matter who I love on this earth, my love for them must not surpass my love for my heavenly Father. If it does then I become an idolater. It would be like me falling in love with my husband's reflection instead of the real person. I would be left rather lonely with only his cold image to talk to. That image could not hold me and speak to me; that image could not help me when I needed it to.

Loving them would not ultimately save me.

And so it was with my own family relationships at the time. Loving them helped me hang on just a bit longer. But loving them would not ultimately save me. I needed to get at the root of all love—to the source of all relationships, the shining relationship from which all other relationships stem.

My most beloved relationships at some point fell short of what my heart truly longed for. Living for your family isn't strong enough to hold you up in certain seasons. And that season for me would change soon.

Into the Half-Light

I feel I am caught in a place for which I was not made. Yet God equips me to carry his brilliance even though I see but dimly through the glass, the fractured glass of a world that thirsts even for a portion of his brilliance. I live and dance in the half-light. I am a shadow chaser.

Timothy Willard

10

The Reason
I'm Alive

*R*ampage, rampage, rampage! The world didn't care! It was all *their* fault. She lumped me into it as well. Rampage, rampage, rampage.

"If you hadn't gotten into so much trouble in school!"
Rampage and more hysterics.
"Too much stress—you cause so much stress."

I came here to get better. I thought since my grandparents had some money, I wouldn't be such a burden in their house. After the last violent family outburst while living at my mom's, the police counseled me to move out. I was sixteen years old. They told me that if my grandmother was willing to take me, then I should live with her in Mississippi. They told me my mother didn't want me causing drama in her house with my younger siblings anymore.

But even though what they said made sense, I needed someone else to tell me that leaving would be okay. All I wanted was to help my brothers and sisters, and I didn't see how my leaving was going to fix anything for them. My stepdad asked the officers if he could talk to me in private. As much as I didn't trust cops, they seemed genuinely concerned about our family and allowed Michael and me some privacy. My stepdad's long, curly hair hid his face while he talked with his head down. When things were serious it was hard for him to look me in the eyes. I know it was because he loved me so much and he didn't want to cry.

"Lacey, there is something I learned when I went to rehab. I want to share it with you."

He handed me a bronze coin with writing on it. I looked down to read it as he recited what it said by heart.

"God grant me the serenity to accept the things I cannot change, courage to change the things I can, and wisdom to know the difference."

I felt like I had left one sad place only to make things worse in another.

"So, what does that mean?" I asked him.

"It means," he said as he pulled me into his arms and wrapped me up in the familiar smell of his leather jacket mixed with cigarettes and motorcycle exhaust, hugging me with all his heart, "that this is one of those times that you can choose to change things. I know you don't want to leave the little ones. But I'll be here to help look after them while your mom works. And I don't want you to go, because I'm gonna miss you a lot. The hard truth is, sometimes we have to stop and help *ourselves* before we are even able to help anyone else."

"So you think I should go then?"

"I think you should go . . . and get better."

So that's why I was here, at Granny's. I came here to get better. I was a thousand miles from my brothers and sisters, who my mom seemed to think were better off without me around. But now, in this barrage of hysterics from my grandmother, I felt like I had left one sad place only to make things worse in another.

I'm sure she didn't mean what she said, but her words painfully wedged their way into my already tired and pain-filled heart. *I might as well be an orphan*, I thought.

And I felt that way. I did. An eerie feeling of being an orphan passed over me. Granny was drunk with pain and continued to vent her fears and hurts. I listened closely for her to confirm the overwhelming thought tormenting me: *The world would be better off without me.* She didn't have to actually say anything close to the phrase, "You're better off dead," for me to manipulate everything she said until it sounded that way in my head. I looked for reasons to give up. I looked for "noble" reasons. All my rationalizing was always done in order to make me "noble" in my own mind.

I could not remember the last time I had fallen asleep without crying. That night I tallied up all the times I had made life harder on the people around me and concluded I was more of a burden than anything else. I talked myself into believing that I was making life worse for everyone.

I was so tired of feeling pain all the time. I wanted it to go away for good.

Being an atheist, I didn't see any reason to keep waking up if I wasn't happy. I tried to keep myself happy and nothing lasted. Everything led to an empty place. As I lay there, I was relieved to have figured out how to make my death something noble: my death would make things easier on everyone. I made myself believe that lie.

I made a plan to commit suicide the next day.

My Plan

I would go to school for a little bit. Hug my girlfriend. She and I had started as friends—friends for years. But we had been dating now for about a month. Our shallow friendship had developed depth when she barely made it through some intense family dysfunction. I happened to be around when some of her worst living nightmares surfaced. I was the only one in her life who knew about the abuse she endured. After those experiences we both came away with a general hatred toward men. We became closer as time went on and we partied together. Eventually our friendship became romantic and she clung to me to help her through. It felt good to be needed at first, but eventually she started to become jealous in a way that proved to me that I was not equipped to carry her life in my hands. It was too much weight for me to be her god, and I felt guilty that I couldn't keep her alive by myself. I knew that it would take a miracle to heal what she was going through, and I also knew that, as much as I wished I could help her somehow, it was clear that I was not that miracle.

Next, there were a few people I wanted to tell off.

After that, I'd leave school and walk home to Granny's house. Granny was supposed to be at the hospital with Gramps. I wished that I was brave enough to go see Gramps in the hospital, but at that time I was terrified to see him that way. He has always been so important to me.

Granny and Gramps used to own a houseboat. Once, when I was four, I was stepping onto the boat and fell into the small

102

space between the dock and the boat. I was drowning when Gramps jumped in and saved me.

He was the best listener. He had a practical wisdom and a deep genius that made life seem limitless when I talked to him. He was also a safe place. When the world was falling apart, I could sit beside Gramps, and even if he didn't say a word, I felt better. The last time I'd seen him, he'd driven me to school. Granny and I had just had a bad argument and I knew I was wrong for the way I acted. When I got in the car beside Gramps, he said nothing to me. But his silence was a relief. Somehow his wordlessness let me know that he knew I knew I was wrong. He gave me grace with his silence. By the time we reached the school, the quiet refuge of the car ride beside Gramps was exactly what I needed to get my head straight. As I opened the door to get out, I said, "Thanks, Gramps."

"I love you, Lacey," he said back. I needed that so much. His love was so believable.

When Granny vented her fears that day, she made me believe Gramps was never coming home from the hospital. I tried my best not to think about it when I came home from school and he was in the hospital. But Granny made it seem like he was already gone and was never coming back. It was too much. So since I knew that the day after our fight Granny would not be home during the day, the house would be empty and open for me to carry out my plan.

When I woke up that morning, I couldn't remember falling asleep. But I did remember that today was to be the last time I would wake up.

Suicide Day

I arrived at my third-period class. I saw a girl who talked trash about me all the time—she didn't know that I knew. She walked by me, reached out her hand, and touched my hair.

103

"You have beautiful hair," she said.

"I hate you," I returned. "I hate you for saying that. I hate your shallowness."

I didn't want to carry the constant pain of my life in my heart anymore.

I hated myself for having long hair because if there was anything beautiful about it, it misrepresented me. I was terrible and worthless on the inside, but no one cared about that. No one knew. This girl cared about hair and nails and shoes—that's it. I hated her for that.

So I grabbed the scissors from my teacher's desk, went to the bathroom, and cut off all my hair. Already it was too much to stay at school and face people any longer. I interrupted my plan of telling people off and walked out of school, and went straight home.

I didn't want to carry the constant pain of my life in my heart anymore.

The Joke That Saved Me

"What are you doing home? What happened to your hair? Answer me!"

I didn't.

Granny should have been at the hospital with Gramps like she said she was going to be, but she wasn't. She was home. When I walked in the door I headed straight for the backyard where I was allowed to smoke. But she saw me and stopped me.

"Please, leave me alone. I just wanna smoke," I said. That's when she snatched the pack of cigarettes out of my hand.

"No. And you aren't smoking anymore. That's it."

Something about her doing this really sent me into a meltdown. Smoking felt like the only thing I had left in the world, and she wanted to take it. I lost it.

"Gramps bought me those because *you* said I was allowed to smoke! I'm losing my mind! I need a cigarette! Give them back! Please, just leave me alone so I can smoke! That's all I'm asking. Please!"

I threw all of the pain of my heart into this issue of her taking my cigarettes so that I could deflect her from the fact that I was really losing it because she was getting in my way. She was interrupting my plan just by being home. But she saw straight through my irrational screaming fit over cigarettes. That's when she began to scream back at me. Her voice has a particular way of cutting through anything.

"Something's wrong with you! You're going to church!"

"No, I'm not. Church is for fake, hypocritical, naïve people who don't know anything about anything! Church is a joke!"

I can't remember what she said after that, but she said it for an hour in the loudest, sharpest, highest pitched tone I could ever remember hearing up to that point in my life. I finally made a simple, rational decision. I did not want to spend my last day on earth listening to this woman scream at me this way. In order to get her to shut up, I told her I would go to church.

It was a Wednesday, so they were having an evening service at Pass Road Baptist Church. Granny was not "dressed appropriately," so she didn't come in. She dropped me off at the front doors and parked right there so that she could make sure I didn't run away.

I sat in the back row in the corner as far away as I could from anything or anyone. I slouched down and closed my eyes, wishing it would hurry up and be over. I had a prejudice against southern accents and thought of Mississippians as unintelligent because of the way they talked. So when the preacher, Brother Edgar, trolled on with his thick southern twang, I hated him.

Then he stopped talking. Right in the middle of his speech, he stopped.

"The Lord wants me to change direction with the topic here," he twanged. "The Lord wants me to talk about families."

He began to talk about different families he'd pastored over the years and, strangely, he began to spell out my life.

It was like the room was empty and he was talking directly to me. It creeped me out. When he finally finished his strangely personal sermon, the room was very quiet. That's when he began to cry. I'd never seen an old white-headed man cry before, so I was riveted. Ignorant, sexist, bigoted rednecks didn't cry.

But I was the hateful one. I was the one flinging my prejudice around. And there I sat, eyes and ears fixed on this old man who was crying like someone he loved had just died or was about to. His sensitivity to God's heart and his humility infiltrated me and all my barriers. He continued to weep with genuine love.

"There is a suicidal spirit in the room," he said through his sobs. The congregation sat, silent.

This is freaking me out, I thought to myself. Goosebumps popped up all over my skin. *I have to get out of this place!*

But I couldn't move until it was all over because Granny was waiting right outside the doors, and if I bolted now everyone would think it was me who had the suicidal spirit! Then other people started crying with the pastor. I heard sniffling all over.

"Please, child," he said, pleading. "Come up here and let us pray for you. God has a plan for your life, and he doesn't want you to die tonight. *Please* come up here and let us pray for you, whoever it is. Please come."

There was no way I was going to go up to the front of the church, in front of all these Christians, and admit I had a problem they thought they could fix. My pride held me down. So I didn't move. And no one went up. And it looked like Brother Edgar may have gotten it wrong. So he asked for people who had been dealing with depression to come up for prayer, and some did.

With the pressure off, the music leader dismissed the church. Finally, I was able to get out of there. I bolted for the door—and right in the doorway a man reached out and gently grabbed my arm. His gentleness was shocking, but when I saw his face I was even more shocked.

God Speaks

My mother always taught me to be suspicious of strange men. She warned me that most of them were perverts and I couldn't trust any of them. It was a sad prejudice my mother taught me, one I continued to learn through my own life. I had my own experiences and things I had witnessed that made me hate men, and I didn't really need my mom's warning. I had seen men sexually and physically abuse people I loved, steal from their struggling families to feed drug and alcohol addictions, break promises to me and my siblings and my mother, and I'd seen seemingly nice, intelligent men turn into drunk, greedy, perverted monsters. A man had assaulted every woman I knew.

So when I looked into this man's face I saw something I'd never seen from a strange older man like him. I saw *pure* love. It was just like how I would picture Jesus looking at someone.

107

He looked at me like he knew me. Like he saw my heart and all its pain. The compassion in his eyes was arresting.

This strange man held me in place with a look that conveyed his genuine, humble, selfless love for me. And I couldn't go anywhere because I didn't know this man and was completely perplexed by why and how he could love me. I waited for him to speak. He'd been crying, so he paused and steadied his voice.

> The compassion in his eyes was arresting.

"The Lord wants me to speak to you," he said. "He wants you to know that even though you have never known an earthly father, he will be a better father to you than any earthly father could ever be."

How could he know? How could he know my feeling of being orphaned? I fought to rationalize his mystical ability of knowing I'd never had a father.

Well, look at yourself, Lacey, I thought to myself. *You have a Metallica shirt on and raggedy, chopped-off purple hair. You don't look like you fit in here and most misfits have daddy issues. He just guessed right is all.*

"God has a great plan for your life," he continued. "You have been questioning your sexuality as well, and the further you go down that road the further you will go from the plan God has for you. This road brings so much pain with it."

Wait, what? Is he talking about my girlfriend? There is no way he could know about that. He kept going.

"God has seen you cry yourself to sleep at night. He has seen you rehearsing the pain you have gone through since you were a little child. You saw too much too soon and it has caused so much pain in your heart. Jesus died to take that pain away. There is pain in your heart from your own sin, and from other people's sins that have affected you. Jesus died on a cross to suffer the consequences of sin forever. That way we don't have to carry that pain around with us. Do you want me to pray for you and ask Jesus to take that pain away?"

Every time he said the word pain it was like my heart broke into a million pieces. I was melting, desperate for anything to make the pain go away.

I nodded, shocking myself by my consent.

He laid his hand on my shoulder and began to pray.

"Heavenly Father, wrap your arms around this girl who you created, like the loving Father you are." As he prayed, a great warmth wrapped around me. I felt a sense of holiness I had never felt before in my life, like God was embracing me. It felt familiar.

It felt like I was finally home.

11

THE REASON
I'm Beautiful

To see beauty we must close our eyes, for it is far beyond what our eyes perceive. I know this now because I received a new vision of myself in the flash of a prayer, in the spark of a thought, in the gasp of a breath. That prayer changed me in so many ways, but stark in my mind is the new perspective it gave me about myself. When you encounter God *for real* so much about your life and thoughts changes.

No one had to say anything about God to me in that moment, because I was encountering him for myself. It was as if I was standing in front of God. *The* God. It was so clear to me this was the only God, the King of everything. The first thing I noticed was his perfect holiness.

There was an order to my thought process, although somehow it all happened in the same moment. First, I saw *myself*.

According to my own moral code, I had considered myself a pretty good person. Compared to the people I hated, I thought I was at least much better than they were. But when you're standing in front of God, saying "I'm good," it's like saying "I'm tall" when you're standing in front of a mountain, "I'm big" when you're standing in front of the ocean, or "I'm old" while looking at the stars. The thought is absurd. I realized that I had no idea what good was, because up to that point I had not stood in the presence of the God who made the universe.

My ideas of love were only shadows compared to this painfully bright, shining, true love that fell all around me.

Then it was like my life flashed before my eyes and I saw everything I had ever done wrong in an instant. I saw all my sins, and no one had to tell me what a sin was and what it wasn't because it was very clear in that moment. I almost wanted to shrink away because I knew I had no right to be in the presence of this infinitely good, perfect, holy God. *This* God was perfect love.

The worst realization was that my idea of love was not really love at all, and because I didn't know true love I had never loved anyone, and even if someone truly loved me I was never able to receive love from them because I could not recognize it. I knew all my ideas of love were only shadows compared to this painfully bright, shining, true love that fell all around me.

All the love I thought I had in me was nothing like *true* love. It was conditional, confused, and even hateful compared to the love I felt God lavishing on me. I felt a great sense of regret and remorse. I felt so sorry for the way I had treated others—how I had hated them. To know I'd been so full of hate and now stood before a God who was love nearly made me collapse from the shame. His holy and loving presence overwhelmed me and sorrow welled up inside me, for his goodness exposed me to myself. My regret was thick, but not thick enough to keep his love from piercing me.

My reaction was a feeling of expectation mixed with a strange longing. I expected God to say to me, "Go away from me forever." And in the strangest way I longed for him to say that to me. It was as if I understood I should be dead, or explode, or just disappear while experiencing the holiness of God. I felt like I was shrinking away, wincing with agony, as I waited for this good God to speak words of justice to me. I knew that if he would cast me away forever, it would be right. And in the presence of God, I was somehow painfully aware of what was right and was overwhelmingly compelled to want what was right.

But at the same time the horror of my true self was revealed to me, I sensed God reacting to me and was surprised when I realized he wasn't casting me away but rather drawing me in closer. It was like he was saying, "Yes, I know you. I know all the things you have done. I am not shocked by any of it. Come close to me, my love, just like you are. I have already forgiven your past and future. And, if you let me, I will make you new. I will make you into all that I have planned for you. You are beautiful, my love."

Where Beauty Hides

I felt that, on that day, I really understood beauty from God's perspective. Our culture focuses so much on what we look like and the things we accumulate. I grew to hate culture for those exact reasons. But in what I felt was my justified indignation with culture, I adopted my own set of rules. *I* defined acceptance, success, goodness, and beauty. I was just

113

as guilty as the prude, or the redneck, or the Christian—all those whom I felt had put their definitions on everyone else.

Beauty, I realized, lay first in our createdness. God created you and me in *his* image. We reflect *his* glory. To all of a sudden realize I was not an accident, a burden, or a mistake but rather intentionally created by a God of holiness, love, and purity changed everything. As I recognized the majesty of God, I began to understand, as he wrapped his arms around me, that I was his creation. I was his idea. From my hair color to my shoe size, from my sense of humor to my taste buds, I was his beloved creation. He knew me better than I knew myself.

And, being a girl he created, I was his daughter. I was in my createdness the daughter of the King of the kings. In this sense I was a princess.

What's more, we are all a mysterious kind of spiritual royalty, for you and I are created by the King of everything. C. S. Lewis talks about this in *The Weight of Glory* when he says: "There are no ordinary people. You have never talked to a mere mortal."[1] I came to meditate on the idea of being a spiritual princess much later in my relationship with God, but when I first came into a relationship with Christ, it was as simple as this: there exists an infinitely good God who created the universe, and he also created me. I am a wonder made by God. A quote I love by St. Augustine says:

1. C. S. Lewis, *The Weight of Glory, and Other Addresses*, rev. and expanded ed. (New York: Macmillan, 1980), 19.

People travel to wonder
at the height of the mountains,
at the huge waves of the seas,
at the long course of the rivers,
at the vast compass of the ocean,
at the circular motion of the stars,
and yet they pass by themselves
without wondering.[2]

Too often we don't recognize our beauty because we won't acknowledge that a loving God made us. It is in this, our createdness, that we find our beauty, our wonder.

The next thing that makes us beautiful is God's unwavering gaze at *us*. We can blaspheme that image of perfect love and holiness by being our hateful, perverted, sinful selves—like I did—but God keeps his eyes fixed on us. I tremble at this thought: he does not turn away from us. He sees us inside and our every sin in all its horror, and he forgives us. He took our sins upon himself when he became a man called Jesus, and he was crucified once and for all, for the sins of the whole world. We are *forever forgiven*. Because I stand forever forgiven I am always beautiful to God. I could finally see myself through his love.

> Although forgiveness and true love were outstretched before me all my life, it wasn't until I chose to believe it that I could actually receive it.

A musician and speaker I love named Christa Black wrote a book called *God Loves Ugly and Love Makes Beautiful*. That phrase by itself was something I understood so profoundly in these first moments of encountering God. So, although forgiveness and true love were outstretched before me all my life, it wasn't until I chose to believe it that I could actually receive it.

2. Augustine, *Confessions* (Oxford: Oxford University Press, 1998), 187.

God sees us all as beautiful and lovely enough to forgive, even though it meant he had to be crucified. The only way to blot out sins in eternity was for God to do that himself, and the only way he could be merciful and just at the same time was to suffer the just consequence of our sin *himself*. God looks at you and me and finds us worth dying for. Forgiveness was a gift bought for me by the blood of Jesus. He offers the same gift to the world.

Beauty, I realized, lay in forgiveness. I found that when I saw myself through God's lens of forgiveness, all my dirt and grime and muck washed away. I saw myself true and translucent, naked and unafraid. I found myself beautiful because God found me forgiven.

How can I explain to you your deep worth and beauty? And no, you don't need to be a girl to be beautiful. And that's just it, isn't it? The beauty of the individual has nothing to do with gender; it doesn't have to do with culture or nationality; it doesn't have anything to do with our sexual impulses. God made us all, and his love leads us toward truth—the truth of ourselves, the truth of others, and the truth about him. When we grasp that truth, we do not grasp a vision of prettiness, but a vision of *worth*. Although I don't deserve it, I am somehow worth God sending his Son to die for me, and so are you. You're beautiful because God sees you as beautiful, and if I had the honor of meeting you, you would know that I see your beauty too.

> I found myself beautiful because God found me forgiven.

12

THE REASON
People Matter

I was not supposed to have woken up. Waking up on the day after I planned to commit suicide was not part of my plan. I remember the moment my eyes opened to the new morning. I could *see*.

There was a clarity that hadn't been there for as long as I could remember. Not a clarity like when you understand something, but the clarity of a blank canvas. The clarity of a flyleaf page in a new book.

If you don't look at the cover, you can't know if the flyleaf is the one in the front or the back of the book. You can't know if it is the end of the story or the beginning. I think each flyleaf is always both. That's what my blank ceiling reminded me of when I opened my eyes that morning. It was a strange thing to feel like I had died yesterday, just like

I wanted to. But I hadn't planned on waking up. I hadn't planned on feeling resurrected from the dead world I had "lived" in for so many years.

So what now? I knew God was in my room that morning. Nothing physically about my room was different from yesterday. The little Christmas tree I kept up all year was still blinking its multicolored lights in the corner. My dresser was still cluttered with overflowing memory boxes. Dimebag Darrell's picture was still tacked on the wall beside my bed.

The only thing different was me.

I stared at the ceiling, thinking about how phenomenal it was that the very God I had hated so much had intervened in my life at the exact moment I was about to throw away the life he gave me. My heart grew warm as I thought about it, until tears streamed from my eyes. It made me cry to think that God was not only real, but that he wasn't far away. He didn't just make life and then watch the pieces randomly and chaotically fall where they may. He was involved. I never would have believed that if I hadn't experienced the presence of God so tangibly the night before. The man who prayed for me spoke so specifically to me and about me. "He has seen you cry yourself to sleep at night," he'd said. That amazed me, humbled me, and comforted me.

"Well, I wasn't supposed to wake up today," I spoke out loud to the God who had saved my life. "So . . . why am I still here? Why did you save me? What do you want from me today?"

Leaves Falling from Trees

I lay awake for hours, just thinking. When it came time to eat breakfast I wasn't hungry, and asked permission to walk to school instead. October had brought its normal relief from the Mississippi heat and I kicked down the road, on my way.

As I turned the corner at the end of our block, I dug through my bag to find the lone cigarette I had stashed in the pocket of my notebook. I hid it there since Granny didn't allow me to bring cigarettes to school. A row of trees to my left, an empty church to my right, all looked on as the tobacco flared into a glow. The air felt different. It seemed so perfect on my bare arms. It seemed thoughtfully measured as it played with my hair. But my cigarette clashed with the perfection of the breeze around me. The same birds that always mocked my dreaded mornings now sang songs of celebration, like they knew it was my birthday—their coronation of my new physical and spiritual life rose into the autumn beauty.

Here's a new daughter! What glory! Oh, the wonder of the great things that are in store for her! they sang.

I felt the wonder of their song. It was everywhere.

It began to overwhelm me, and I dropped my head to turn away from the undeserved kindness of the gentle wind kissing my face. When I looked down I noticed the golden leaves I'd been walking on. Then I looked up at the evergreens and wondered where all the leaves I'd been trampling on had come from. *They could have traveled very far*, I thought. The idea of their origin plagued me. I imagined they had followed the wind all the way from somewhere I could never picture myself going, like

119

New York. Then I thought, *But* God *knows where each leaf came from.* The thought surprised me and made me giggle with the idea there was a real person like God who knew not only what state each leaf had come from, but what tree and seed, and when and where that seed fell, and how long it took to grow, and on and on and on back to the moment he created trees.

God knew.

And he knew the exact moment the leaf I was standing on fell, and why. I stopped walking and stared at the leaves. I began to laugh at the romance of it all. The mystery and beauty and wonder of an ancient, intricate, creative, thoughtful, mathematical, brilliant, artistic, playful God.

> I began to laugh at the romance of it all. The mystery and beauty and wonder of an ancient, intricate, creative, thoughtful, mathematical, brilliant, artistic, playful God.

How immense and overwhelming! My mind struggled to grasp the fact there was a living God who still made trees grow, lose leaves, and spread seeds. I laughed at the beauty of God and fell a little more in love with him.

Understanding Love and God's Art

The first thing I understood about this new place or state in which I now existed was that God wanted me to know he loved me. It was as if he kept reminding me he loved me with breezes of joy randomly tickling my heart all day long. I believe this was the first time I encountered joy. Joy is not mere happiness. It's as if happiness comes from our souls, but joy comes from the spirit within our souls. Joy was a beautiful and astonishing melody singing in my heart all about how much God loved me.

Next, I realized how much God cared about other people. He wanted me to know this about him so I would learn from him and do the same—he wanted me to love others the way he did. At school that day, I would see someone I had hated yesterday and have to walk away from her because I would start to cry with an understanding of how much God loved her.

I remember sitting in the lunchroom, alone in the corner, and just looking at everyone. I was one day into my new love affair with God. I fell in love with him because he'd been so supernatural, powerful, and present, and mostly because he gave me grace by loving me enough to embrace me as I was. And because I was so enchanted by the love of God, I wanted to know more about him. As I looked at the lunchroom full of people, I had a revelation of God saying something very simple about all of them: *This is my artwork. These are my masterpieces.*

I began to cry when I understood that the God of holiness, love, and mercy I'd met yesterday had made every person in that room. This was especially sweet for me to understand, because my favorite thing to do when I made a friend or started to have a crush on someone was to explore their artwork. I knew that people's art, whatever kind of art it was, said something about the deepest part of who they were. I always knew that seeing people's art would make me fall even more in love with them. You could always see the artist's fingerprints in the art, like their signature.

To suddenly see people as God's art overwhelmed me with humility. I had hated people so much. I had oversimplified them; I had judged, condemned, ridiculed, perverted, abused, and used them. It was like I'd spent so much time spitting on God's art and calling it worthless. It broke my heart to understand this.

"Oh, my God. Forgive me," I said under my breath.

121

Not long after that, my girlfriend, Amanda, came over and sat by me at the lunch table.

"Oh, you cut your hair. I'm not gonna lie, it kinda looks like crap. You're probably gonna need to wear a hat for a while." She laughed. "Too bad they don't let us wear hats in school."

Then she started cussing our assistant principal because the rules seemed stupid and made no sense to her.

As she talked I was in awe of how Amanda's life said something about who God was. She was God's creation. I became so fascinated by this revelation that I just stared at her.

I noticed the way her freckles—which she despised—looked as random and enchanting as the stars in the universe. God had put them there.

I noticed the way her eyes were moving so quickly around the room and perceiving so much. Eyes are amazing. God made them.

I noticed the way she bit into her apple and realized how crazy it was that we had taste buds. I thought about how I gave my dog the same dry dog food every day, but God gave us taste buds and all kinds of different flavors of food to eat. It seemed so loving of him. He made taste buds.

"Why are you looking at me like that?" she asked.

I had no idea where to start.

How do I explain? I thought.

I remembered what the guy at church had said to me about my relationship with Amanda. In that moment, I understood that God wanted me to love her and let her go. If it wasn't God's best for me to have this kind of relationship, then it wasn't God's best for her either. God had something better for both of us. It was a subtle feeling, but I knew God wanted me to really love her like he did in that moment.

I told her, "I'm just thinking about a lot, is all."

"What are you thinking about?" she asked.

"I don't know how to explain it right now. I'm sorry. Let's talk about it later."

I excused myself and went to the bathroom to cry alone. I sat in the bathroom and, for a few minutes, just processed the fact that God made everyone and loved them all. All day as I thought about it and felt the truth of it deep in my heart, it would overwhelm me and drive me to tears.

God loves everyone.

He made everyone.

Each person has his fingerprints on them. Each person's life says something about who God is. He is so vast that if all the grains of sand and stars in the sky were alive to say something amazing about God, it would not be close to saying all the good there is to say about who he is. I find myself, even now, living in the glow of thankfulness for such a magnificent and all-powerful God.

When I arrived home from school that day, Granny returned my cigarettes.

"Your Gramps is doing better today. Thank you for going to church yesterday. You look a lot better. I love you, Lacey."

I just thanked her and took the cigarettes. I sat outside smoking, thinking about everything that had changed inside of me. I didn't tell Granny. Not yet. That night I lay in bed and listened as Billy Corgan sang about how life was changing. "What is love?" he asked. He didn't like change; he was afraid of it. I thought about my desperation. I had wanted something—anything—to change so badly I was ready to die over it. But I couldn't imagine anything different than what I had known. Life outside of my grungy cave of bitterness and hate was completely foreign to me. It was mysterious, like a blank canvas in my mind. Kind of like looking at the ocean for the first time and being unable to imagine what kind of world exists inside it.

Our Decisions Define Us

I think so many people get Christianity wrong, and it makes me sad. It's viewed as a religion of dos and don'ts. God cares about our hearts and the state of our souls. He wants us in relationship with him. God wants us to have life, and only he, the Creator of life itself, can tell us the truth about the difference between life and death. The One who formed our spirit within us is the One who knows what is poison to our spirit and what is healthy for it.

> God wants us to have life, and only he, the Creator of life itself, can tell us the truth about the difference between life and death.

Whenever God would point out something in my life that I was holding back from him, he was always so gentle with me about it. He was always so loving when he would ask me to let him into something in my heart that I'd rather keep him out of. And it was as if he always left it up to me. He was and continues to be so very kind and patient.

I remember how God started to squeeze my heart whenever I thought about my relationship with Amanda. It was one of the first major decisions I had to make after my encounter with God to really choose him. I knew that I'd be dead if he hadn't saved my life. I knew that if I ended my relationship with Amanda, I would have to be very distant friends with her, if we could even stay friends at all. Deeply emotional romantic relationships are the most difficult things to walk away from, and "staying friends" can create unhealthy cycles. I wasn't sure how she would take what I had to tell her.

I knew that if I were going to die tomorrow, the short time on earth I had left before I got to eternity had to be spent saying yes to whatever God was calling me to. I also knew how much deeper and more perfectly God loved Amanda than I ever could. God had saved my life, so the least I could do in return was give it to him for whatever he wanted. So I decided to talk to Amanda about what had happened in my life and let her know that I couldn't date her anymore. It would be much better for Amanda to hear about my encounter with God than for her to hear about my death by suicide.

She came over and we sat on the floor in my room. I cried as I explained what had happened. She cried as she heard it. She cried at my suicidal wish and my salvation. She cried about the experience I had with God. She understood about my wanting to live my life differently, my desire to live for eternity instead of just for this life that was passing and so short. She understood that we had to end our relationship. She cried with me and we were both sad, but we were both happy too. God had so much grace on my life to know what I could handle at that time. It was his miracle that she was so understanding.

I'm thankful that Amanda and I were able to end that way. Years later there were other relationships that had to end as well, but those stories I'll save for another book, another conversation with you, dear reader. Just know this: I had to trust God with someone threatening suicide in order to obey him by leaving the situation. But God was so sweet to me to let this one come easy.

My New Vision

There's a well-known Bible verse in 1 John 4:19 that says you and I should love because God first loved us. How beautiful and tender of the awe-inspiring God I encountered in that Baptist church to love me first—to love me enough to come after me. And it's reciprocal. Though he doesn't need it, he desires my affection as well.

But God's love goes so much further. When you and I realize the depth of his love, he then desires us to love others the way we ourselves are loved by him. The great philosopher Søren Kierkegäard says that love begins in a vertical line, what I would call a vertical dimension. This love affair begins with God first loving us, and that love then empowers us, inspires us, and guides us into loving others. The vertical finds its way into the horizontal, and suddenly we're able to see past the shadows and into the real core of one another; we're able to see people the way God sees them—as fearfully and wonderfully made.

God's love spoke to me about a relationship I needed to confront in my own life: my relationship with Amanda. He had something better for each of us. If you would have told me when Amanda and I started dating that I would be the mother of two thriving little boys and the wife of a loving husband, I would have laughed in your face and probably cussed you out for good measure. I didn't ever want to have kids, and I had such a sad hatred toward men. But the history of our lives reveals God's enduring plan. We look back and see all along he had something better for us, something more wonderful, something in line with his greater plan for the entire human race. Something that is not based on fear but rather destroys fear with trust. Something that isn't based on old wounds but rather heals them through forgiveness and faith.

Was it hard to talk to Amanda? Yes. But many times goodness in life is appreciated only after trudging through the muddy bogs of our own shortsighted choices. And there, on the other side of the stench, we find the shining gem of the life we were intended to live. It shines because it's on fire with God's holiness. But it doesn't burn us. Rather, it galvanizes our hearts and minds and souls, enabling us to love—to bring the vertical into the horizontal and discover how we were meant to live.

13

THE REASON

I Sing

As far as I know, my mother was born with her old nylon string classical guitar in hand. She's played it ever since I can remember. And whether in our house or in our car, my mother always had music playing. I could sketch out on paper the soundtrack to my early life. I suppose it was inevitable for my siblings and me to all love and make music of some kind growing up.

I believe somewhere there is a picture of me, fourteen years old, sitting on the couch in a T-shirt and baggy pajama pants in front of a Christmas tree, and my mouth is hanging open in shock. Wrapping paper was scattered all over the living room floor and I expected the gift part of the morning to be over. And as my expression explains, I was amazed to see my mom coming around the corner with a bass guitar—held out to me.

I had wanted to play the drums for a while, but I reasoned that if I was going to cart an instrument around to friends' houses, it would probably be a pain to try to carry a drum set.

So I had mentioned to my mom once that I wanted to play the bass, since my brother Eric played guitar already. Eric had a subscription to *Guitar World*, which was the coolest magazine because it had guitar and bass tabs to popular rock songs in the back. I thought my brother was so cool because he knew how to play Weezer, Nirvana, Smashing Pumpkins, Marilyn Manson, and White Zombie songs—all because he had a subscription to *Guitar World*. I wanted to play those songs with him, so I really needed a bass guitar to do that.

When I saw the black Fender jazz bass I sat in shock because I didn't think we could afford something like that. But there it was, along with a sparkling, fuzzy, purple strap. I didn't have an amp yet, so I spent the rest of Christmas Day in the bathroom with the headstock resting against the bathtub, with *Guitar World* magazines all over the floor, figuring out bass lines to the songs my brother already knew. That Christmas present really rocked my world.

Beyond My Mind's Limits

I was such a cynic that I could never take anyone's word for anything. I wanted to find out for myself what the Bible said, so I read it all the time. I continued to fall in love with what I read about Jesus and true Christianity in the Bible. And everything I read seemed to say what I was already sensing through my encounters with the Spirit of God in church. It was easy to sense God's Spirit when I was standing in the front row, unable to see anyone behind me, during the praise and worship songs at church. I became extremely addicted to the feeling of God moving in worship.

I've heard people bash that feeling because they label it "emotionalism." I think there is a difference between emotionalism and what I experienced at Pass Road Baptist Church in those early days of being a Christian. This was completely different from some self-help situation. It was beyond my mind's limits. It touched my spirit and, for a while, simply and profoundly opened up the meaning of Christ's death to my heart. I couldn't even say the words "Jesus died for my sins" without weeping, because I was continuously understanding the meaning of that event in a deeper and deeper way.

There is something about music that opens up your soul to understand, to meditate on something, to taste the spiritual significance of the world around you.

The music in the church, sung from the heart and led by the Spirit, seemed to transport me into a timeless zone where angelic worship of the Most High God of the Universe was already happening in eternity. I understood the full power of music in church during worship. This is what music seems meant for, and we are invited to join in through creating and playing and singing to God. Wow.

When God gives you a gift, you can use and abuse your gift however you want. But I believe music was ultimately meant to express God's heart, and to express the heart of others toward God. I believe this because when I experience music in this context, honest, consistent, crazy beautiful, supernatural encounters with God seem to be the normal result.

I understood the great difference between emotionalism and true spiritual encounters when I saw extreme examples in the secular arena. There are emotional blues singers who make you wallow in your sadness, hypersexualized jazz and pop musicians, and romantic country and folk singers, all of whom pull at your heartstrings in order to move you. You can find yourself crying and not even understand the words. There are still other musicians who have a spirit of influence. They can make you chant, dance, and give you the chills, like Rage Against the Machine. And what about punk rock? That's a music genre built around outright rebellion; it makes you want to go fight in the war before you even know what you're supposed to be raging against. And then, beyond emotionalism, there is the demonic spiritual experience in music as well. We love satisfying our emotions because, in my opinion, we are simply dying to feel anything.

After my encounter with God, I went to the Pantera concert that I'd already bought tickets for. The intensity of the genuine hate and anger was absolute emotionalism. It made the audience want to start fights with each other for no apparent reason. Sometime later I stumbled into a crowd on the street that was waiting to hear a band play on the outdoor stage. From the moment this band played the first notes in their set, I felt a great sense of the demonic. It was overwhelming and made me want to vomit. The power of music, with its effect on the soul, is one of the most tangible ways to touch someone's heart or spirit.

I began to be very selective about the music I let into my soul and spirit because of how powerful I knew music could be. Emotions aren't wrong, but letting them control your life and sway all your decisions can be deceptive and very destructive. I felt myself slip easily back into depression and condescension whenever I listened to certain music.

There are seasons when we're more vulnerable to falling back into our old lives than others. For a while, I simply could not continue to listen to the music I had in the past because it haunted me in ways that stole my joy, peace, and the victorious feeling I had over suicide and hatred. But when I would listen to music that was meant to be used to worship God and praise him, I would experience the opposite. It built up my spirit and opened up my heart to learn and grow. I meditated on God through the music, and as long as I did I could sense his presence. The music acted like a doorway into God's throne room.

The Bible says in Psalm 100:4 that we can enter into God's gates with thanksgiving and into his courts with praise. The more I entered in this way, the more intimate my relationship with God became. The more you hang out with someone you love, the more you learn about them, the deeper you *know* them.

> Music acted like a doorway into God's throne room.

In many ways this is what worship music was doing in my heart. As I joined in the congregational singing I experienced just how strong the words, when truly sung from the heart to God, could be. I understood Psalm 22:3, which talks about how the praises of his people enthrone God. I was able to actually experience this verse coming to life.

Unusual Lightness

It really is as if the praise and worship music in church pulls back the veil between God and man and lets us actually encounter a foreshadow of heaven, of being in the presence of God. Just like I experienced a physical feeling of nausea in the presence of the demonic, at times there are physical feelings in the presence of God. Everyone describes these feelings differently because everyone's relationship with God is as unique as the individuals God created. For me, there is an unusual lightness in my heart and in my body. I feel a warm burning in my chest and stomach. Sometimes when I'm singing or speaking and I feel like God is helping me, I can hear nothing but a ringing in my ears, like someone hit a bell and I can only hear its sustain.

I feel goosebumps on my skin, along with a sense of crazy peace and joy. In these experiences with God I have a renewed, firm understanding of what the word *awe* means. There's a definite sense of awe in the presence of God, and I experienced this the most in the worship setting in church. I fell madly in love with experiencing awe. This experience was more than emotion. Something within us resonates when we encounter the sublime in life. C. S. Lewis talks about this feeling of awe in his book *The Problem of Pain*. In it he describes the word *numinous*. The numinous is that "thing" we sense or feel that is outside of ourselves.

In Lewis's children's book *The Lion, the Witch and the Wardrobe*, the little girl Lucy asks Mr. Beaver if Aslan the Lion is safe. "Of course he's not safe," replies Mr. Beaver, "but he is good." The idea of something, or in the case of God, *someone*, not being safe but good is the feeling of the numinous. He is awesome, and not cute and fuzzy awesome but rather tremendously awe-inspiring—a God who is altogether good and altogether beautiful.

God was so gracious to me in that season of my life to always meet me this way whenever I would turn my heart toward him in this setting. Later I would come to realize that I can't love God just for the experience of worship any more than I would want my husband to love me just for the feelings he got when we made love. Having a relationship with God means so much more than just trying to find the goosebumps. But for me, turning my heart toward God seemed to consistently bring the goosebumps, so it was difficult at first to know that the experience and the relationship were different things.

There have been seasons when I couldn't feel much of anything, and times when being in a relationship with God challenged me and felt more like a weight than the freedom that it truly is. But as with any relationship we care deeply about and want to last, I chose to continue trusting the beautiful God I encountered so powerfully, even when it felt like he was far away.

Most of the time, in these moments, it was me who was far away, even though God wanted to pull me close. But as with parents and children, sometimes the parent must let the child go for a time. How else will they learn to walk? How else will they learn to eat solid food if the parent does not let them hunger for more than milk? How else will they learn balance if the parent does not allow them to fall down? But this first intensely romantic season with God was important for me to be able to trust him. It taught me how to long for intimacy and what it feels like to desire God "like the deer pants for the stream of water," as King David wrote about in Psalm 42:1. The harder seasons came later.

I also had to find a good balance between worshiping by myself and with other people within the church. I could lie on my face in my room and put on worship music and seek him alone. These times proved to be important for me and my spiritual growth. These times also carried revelation and their own kind of awesome encounters. But the times at church brought much-needed confirmation of what I experienced alone, as well as new gifts in other people that expressed who Christ is and what he was saying to me that I couldn't hear on my own.

Christianity was built upon intimate community. Jesus lived with his twelve disciples. They traveled and ate together; they worshiped and discussed things together. Jesus seems to love bringing diverse groups of people together. The church body is the same way. The relational aspect of Christianity cannot be overlooked, and it really spoke to me, especially in the worship context.

So, as much as I needed and loved to worship God on my own in my room, or on the beach, or on the roof during sunrise or sunset, I also needed and loved being in the midst of an assembly of people who were seeking God in united diversity. This is where the most challenge, encouragement, and confirmation in my walk with Christ have always come from.

> I didn't have to control or manipulate anything or anyone. I didn't have to defend myself or be afraid of anything.

There were so many things in my heart that were healed during times of worship in church. I laid out many dark lies in my heart before God's light, so that he could shine on them and expose them for what they were: lies about my identity, my self-worth, my orphaned feelings. I laid so many anxieties to rest. It was here in these moments that I felt free to open my hands, in a sense. It was as if I no longer had to hang on to anything. I didn't have to control or manipulate anything or anyone. I didn't have to defend myself or be afraid of anything.

In these moments of worship, when I laid myself bare, my spirit was ministered to with an ever-increasing understanding of God. I realized how deep the comfort of knowing his sheer magnificence and enormity reached. He is bigger than all my problems. He is good even though so much in the world feels evil. He protects me with love and wisdom. He controls the planets and stars and set them all in order.

And yet he gives you and me the freedom to make bad choices, and even allows us to be affected by the bad choices of others. He can do this because no matter what, he keeps us safe. He works out something glorious even though the bad of it all seems so big and dark. But I have come to understand that the bad has nothing on my God.

If I sat through a thousand sermons that detailed all the good things about God, but didn't spend time worshiping God with my whole heart and spirit and mind, those messages would be forgotten. Worship plays such a vital role in my relationship with God. For it is in those times when you rend your heart and throw it at God's feet that you finally realize how wide and how deep his love really goes. There's freedom that comes with consistently increasing your understanding of who God is, and you can't acquire this knowledge anywhere else. God created us for that special freedom. That's why our hearts ring out when we experience it.

That's why I wanted to be at church every time the doors were opened. Anytime the altar was open to go up and kneel in prayer, I was there, asking God questions I was wrestling with, repenting of things I needed to let go of, asking for strength and wisdom for different situations I was going through. I began to go to church all the time.

My Band, My Voice, God's Miracle

I was still playing in the band Sofa Kingdom for a little while after I became a Christian, but the lyrics seemed like they weren't really true or from my heart anymore. I wasn't as angry about the things I was singing about. I no longer viewed people as wasted space.

So I tried to change the lyrics. That helped a little, but my heart was still changing and it got to the point where I didn't want to go to the parties the band was having, and I didn't want to even listen to the same music they were listening to. I wanted them to know God like I had gotten to know him. I talked to them about what had happened to me. They seemed kind of shocked and happy for me, but I don't think it really stuck with them like it stuck with me.

But something happened that solved everything. I got a tumor in my throat.

A little while after I became a Christian, Granny noticed a lump on my neck. She asked me about it, and I wasn't aware that it was even there. She took me to the doctor and they took some X-rays. Sure enough, there was a tumor growing in my throat.

The doctor sent the pictures to Tulane University in New Orleans, and the doctors there asked me to come to their hospital right away for a biopsy. I went to church before I left, and everyone prayed for me. One woman put her hand on my throat and prayed that I would be completely healed, that the tumor would shrink until it disappeared.

When she had prayed, I reached up and touched my neck where the lump was and it was gone. I started crying and knew that God had healed me right then. I went to Tulane that next morning, and they had the original X-rays with the picture of the tumor. They took some new ones and could not find the tumor at all.

They kept asking the nurse if she was sure she had the right X-rays. They compared the pictures and stood there amazed. My tumor was completely gone.

When I returned to church that next Sunday, the music leader was on the keyboards playing this song to which everyone always danced.

The words rang out with joy about how we should get up and praise and thank God if he had been good to us. The worship leader bounced his hands on the keyboard with such freedom as he led the congregation in declarations about how God had set us free in so many ways.

The joy of this song, being so true in my heart and explaining my experience so sweetly, filled my heart until that joy overflowed. It always overwhelms me to acknowledge, "Yes,  God, you are good and you are real, and you care about every square inch of our lives." I had read about Jesus healing people in the Bible, and I had read where he told the people who believed in him to go and heal in his name. I believed so much when I read it, but I had never seen it play out in my own life. So this moment of praising God was very special to me.

I was dancing around the church, thanking God for healing me. It was the first healing miracle I had experienced as a Christian. The next thing I knew, the music leader was saying, "If this is your prayer tonight, if you have something to thank and praise God for, then come up here and sing this song to Jesus!" Before I realized what was happening, I was on stage holding the microphone and singing that song with all my heart. I just wanted to thank him so much for healing me.

This was the first time I had ever used my voice to sing in front of people about what God had done in my life. I watched the whole room begin to move. Every person in that room danced with joy as long as I continued to sing. That was when I knew I could never use my voice to sing for anything or anyone except God. He had redeemed me *and* healed my throat, so now it was all for him.

I gave my voice to him that night, and I said, "God, have your way in my singing. You made it, you healed it, and you gave it back to me, so now I give it back to you. It's yours forever. Amen."

I decided to quit Sofa Kingdom.

14

THE REASON
I Wanted to Change
the World

Originally the vision I had for starting a band came from my love for Nirvana. Nirvana came on the scene during one of the most disgustingly materialistic times of this century. The 1980s were all about being vain and having the most expensive, most in, most fashionable *whatever*. If you were a poor kid in the '80s and early '90s, you were pretty much an outcast. So after my years of wearing my brother's ridiculously oversized hand-me-downs from the thrift store and getting relentlessly made fun of by all the pretty girls in nice clothes at school, Nirvana suddenly made this outcast cool. Thank you, Nirvana!

The members of Nirvana were just regular anybodies, but they took the stage and shocked everyone with how heartfelt and amazing their show and sound were. I thought this contrast was beautiful then, and I still do now. They were the antirock stars who showed the world that it was okay to be yourself and hate whatever was popular because, whoever you were, that was the coolest thing to be. They pointed to the heart and away from the outward appearance, which was so inspiring for an awkward, ugly girl like me, who felt life deeply in her heart. They gave a voice to those the world deemed weak and worthless by calling them to sing along, "We have passion! We have passion about not caring what anyone says or thinks!" They were themselves, and because of that they gave everyone, especially the underdogs, permission to be themselves too. They rose to be one of the biggest influences of our generation, and I believe the philosophy they promoted is still changing the world.

If I could bring that experience into a bar, people would experience a longing to live their lives to the full potential for which they were created.

My driving desire to start a band and play the music beating in my heart came from the fact that so much of my life had been changed while I encountered the Spirit of God during the worship music in church. I thought if I could bring that experience into a bar, people would experience a longing to live their lives to the full potential for which they were created.

If I could play loud enough and sing honestly enough with all my heart to God, about what he had done in my life to save me from suicide and death and hell, then God would show up in such a tangible way. And not only would he show up, but he'd do the same thing in the hearts of the desperate people in the room that he'd done in mine. I knew that there was a whole generation of people who had fallen in love with Nirvana for the same reasons I did and felt sympathy for Kurt Cobain's suicide, even to the extent of taking a step closer to dying themselves. I once believed in the death wish of a generation who felt like they were less than others, like they were a burden to the world around them, like they were not important and had no purpose.

So, out of the inspiration I received from Nirvana, combined with the way I was rescued by a living God and saved from suicide, I was determined to assemble a group of unassuming anybodies—*passersby*—who, once they got on stage, blew the roof off of the place.

Pat, our bass player, is a rock star with his instrument, but if I had never seen him play, I would have never called him that. He is exactly the kind of anybody I'm describing—unassuming, polite, and honoring of every human he encounters. He comes from a family of artists and can sit quietly for hours working on his mind-blowing artwork. Pat is also just generally brilliant.

So is Sameer. He is the kind of guy who loves friendship and adventure, and he has a fearlessness that encourages people to be risk takers in cool ways. But he is also an intellectual, nerdy type who loves astronomy and science fiction and is perfectly happy to curl up in a corner with a good book for days. So it is always a little surprising to see his passion pouring unpredictable sounds into his guitar through riffs and progressions that make my heart soar.

Jared, our youngest member, has a mischievous kind of smarts, especially when it comes to pulling pranks. But he also possesses a deep wisdom for his age. Jared would have been happy to stay at home being the best at every video game created, but he could also write tremendous progressive metal songs, and slam into the guitar with a contagious, joyful freedom and a hit-you-in-the-chest kind of crunch.

James builds computers and can fix anything that's broken. He is the kind of person who gives all his time, money, and sleep to help anyone around him with a need. But he also plays like a human metronome and almost perfectly hits the crap out of the drums.

They are all soft-spoken too, perfectly unassuming.

Perfectly unassuming, that is, until the feedback starts on Sameer's guitar. It was at that electric moment we hoped to steal people's breath. In a general way, this is the heart behind the band name we chose: Passerby. Our mission statement said, "We are just a Passerby with a story like anyone else. We want to inspire people to stand up in their purposes and be moved to change the world the way God made each person to change it, in their own unique and very important way."

I still believe in this mission statement. Kurt Cobain had a passion to dismantle the spirit of the age, the selfishness and hatred and materialism that cause narcissism. His legacy in that regard continues. He changed the entire music culture with passion and a brilliant nonchalance that came as spring water to a thirsty culture of nobodies like me.

The Birth of Flyleaf

The scene: it was a typical, clear blue Austin sky. The South by Southwest music festival drew people to Texas from all over the country. New bands, old bands, solo artists, and busking homeless musicians filled the downtown Austin air with music. The smell of Texas barbecue was making my stomach rumble. I hadn't eaten yet, and it was nearly three in the afternoon. But I could never eat before we played in those days.

Our very first show was a battle of the bands event in the youth building of a Methodist church in downtown Temple, Texas. We were the first band of the night. I had copied a makeup trick I learned from another local band with two female lead singers called Animal Couch. I took hair gel and mixed it with a bunch of red glitter, smeared it over my eyelids, and let it dry. I looked like I was a professional battle of the bands contestant now.

Just before the doors opened for the show, the DJ for the headlining band, The Grove, brought in a sack of Whataburger burgers loaded with onions. I hadn't realized how nauseated I was until that moment. It felt like he had shoved those onions right up my nose, and I started to gag. I walked out of the youth building and found the bathroom, and I barely made it in the door before I threw up in the sink. I kept dry heaving after that and was tearing up the whole time. Glitter was sliding down into my eyes and making them water even worse.

"They're opening the doors, Lacey!" someone yelled at me from outside.

My stomach knotted up again, and I dry heaved a few more times before I was able to stand up straight. I caught a glance of myself in the mirror before rushing out. I looked like I had just lost the battle of the bands now. But there was no time to fix anything.

I'll just keep my head down, I thought.

I reached in my pockets and felt the handfuls of tiny red plastic party stars, and I was nervous. *Is this gonna be cheesy? What are the lyrics to the first song? I hope I don't fall on my face. I gotta remember to keep my head down. Why am I doing this?*

"Oh, Jesus." I said out loud. "Help me. I can't do this without you."

Everyone was already on stage. I walked up and Jared and Sameer began the feedback on their guitars. "Red Sam" was our first song. I still felt like I was going to puke.

Help me, help me, help, help, help . . . Oh, Jesus, help me, please. Don't let me puke.

The intro riff ripped from Sameer's guitar, and everything in the building seemed to rise with the notes. I put my hands in my pockets and filled them with those tiny red stars.

Here comes the hit, I thought.

As soon as James had smashed the cymbal I spun around and threw a handful of stars into the air above the kids who were all smashed together at the front of the stage. The second hit came and I flung my arms across them again, sending an arched streak of sparkling stars over them a second time. This time their hands went up—they were reaching for them.

Oh, God bless them, Lord, I prayed. *Especially the ones who struggle with wanting to be alive and not knowing who they are or why they are here. Pour out your love and grace and peace over them, Lord, and let them know that you are close and here and that you care. Tell the devil to shut up, God.*

Then I opened my mouth and sang the first line of the song.

"Here I stand, empty hands . . ."

Right then peace fell over me and my nausea passed.

I knew in that moment I was not going to throw up on the audience.

That was the first time I had gone through the process of preparing mentally for a Passerby show. By now, after a few dozen shows, I was familiar with the process. I knew better than to eat before we played.

Our South by Southwest showcase was an early one, so it wouldn't be that hard to wait. So when my stomach rumbled at the smell of barbecue, I ignored it. My makeup was already done and I didn't want to risk throwing up and crying it all off. Not today. RCA was in the audience. Our friend and manager at the time, Gabriel Colbert, assured us that not only was RCA watching, but so was someone called a music entertainment lawyer, who could help us get signed. He said her name was Monika, and she was already obsessed with our demo. "Broken Wings" was her favorite song. Of course we'd insert that into our playlist just for her.

The sound engineer for the band PushMonkey was brilliant. We'd met him when we opened for them a couple months ago. His name was Rich Caldwell. We didn't have a sound guy to help us that night, so Rich had offered to run sound for our show for free. He liked our set so much that he offered to do it again sometime. Later that night we'd all gone for Taco Bell and Rich had joined us. We laughed over lots of dumb jokes, the dumber the funnier. It was our very own dumb joke–telling contest.

Then Rich had started to talk to me about God. He asked me questions about what we believed and seemed surprised by my answers. He mentioned that it was strange to meet religious people who didn't seem judgmental like other religious people he knew.

"I don't like to say I am religious because it lumps me in with a bunch of people that I don't understand," I'd said. "Instead I just really love Jesus."

He'd tilted his head up and smiled at that, like he had been thinking of just that idea and wondering about the difference.

"We should talk more about this sometime."

"Yes!" I'd answered. "I'd love to. It's my favorite topic."

"Cool!" he said. "Let me know when you are playing again. I'd love to help you guys out when I can."

And so it was Rich at the soundboards once again for South by Southwest. We were all ecstatic that Rich was available to help us out during our set. This was the most important show we had ever played, and Rich made us sound a thousand times better than we really were. And when we played, I could tell from Monika's long, tangled mass of full-bodied hair that was flailing around and her rock horns swung over her head that something about our show was definitely winning her over. We all felt like something exciting was about to happen.

The most encouraging person in the audience was Jared's grandpa, Pop. He stood up above everyone, leaning on the guardrail with his rock fist up the entire set. *Pop thinks we rock*, I thought to myself. *What else really matters?* It made me smile like a goofball.

After the show, Monika, the RCA rep, and a representative from BMI offered to buy us a Stubb's barbecue dinner. We sat there and learned about the music industry from these excited, beautiful women who loved our inexperienced little band. We only played because it was fun, and I think they loved that about us. It made them giddy. And their giddiness made us giddy.

I looked around the table at the guys—teenagers, most of them. I was so thankful to get to do this with them. I knew we were going to be a family for a while after this, and I loved them all so much. I couldn't think of a better group of humble guys to start this adventure with. I wondered what they were thinking. I wondered if they knew what I knew. I wondered if they knew that we were beginning an amazing journey that was going to change all our lives in so many great ways.

15

I Wanted to Go to Hell

We sat around the conference table in the New York City office for Octone Records with about twelve people who would make up our future record label. Our lawyer and manager were with us. By this time we had discovered that the name Passerby was already trademarked by another artist, and so we had changed the name of our band to Flyleaf. We discussed our vision for Flyleaf and the difference between being freely artistic in our music and being universally acceptable. We discussed the ways we'd have to compromise artistically in order to reach a bigger audience.

Suddenly the subject shifted from artistic compromise to the question of how much of a role our faith would play in Flyleaf music. They wanted to know if we were looking to be a Christian band, or simply Christians who were in a band.

For some reason my ears got very hot at this moment and I heard a crazy ringing coming from my brain and filling my ears. I had no idea what was happening except that I was talking, and I knew I was talking about Jesus and hell and music and worship, and about how people need to know that there is hope for them in the face of their deepest hopelessness and pain. I knew that everyone was staring at me, completely engrossed in what I was saying about these things, yet I have no idea what it was that I actually said. But afterward, Octone seemed to still be on board with wanting to sign us.

> I wanted with all my heart to go to those places that are an eerie foreshadow of hell—and pull people out.

The reason we wanted a label that would market us to radio that had no regard for Jesus at all, and the reason we wanted to tour with bands who were atheistic and blasphemous in their lyrics, was because that's where I would find a hopeless girl like myself looking for her real purpose—someone like my sixteen-year-old self who had tremendous pain in her heart and was overwhelmingly tired of living the life she was living.

I wanted with all my heart to go to those places that are an eerie foreshadow of hell—and pull people out.

Singing to Shadows

The club was hot and dark. It smelled like stale beer and cigarettes. A couple screamed at each other in one corner. Two girls made out in another corner. A kid with bloodshot eyes and a goofy smile, who couldn't have been older than fourteen, stood front and center, smoking a cigarette, wearing a shirt with the words "F-Y'all" on the front and "I'm from Texas" on the back. His girlfriend absentmindedly twisted her dark dreadlocks while staring at the blonde girl beside her in disgust. You could see the "Give-me-one-reason-to-slap-you-please-I-can't-wait" look on her face as her eyes burned a hole in the back of the blonde's head. The blonde girl was much too big to be wearing the tight little tube top she had on, and her tiny shorts looked more like underwear. Her high heels provided just enough height for her to see above the stage. She laughed loudly at every male around her who said anything at all, whether it was funny or not.

It was one of our first big shows in Houston.

The opening band had already finished their set. The sound system had cut out for so long that the frustrated lead singer had convinced the crowd to hold their middle fingers in the air and chant profanities at the sound guy. A guy in a leather jacket held his four-year-old son on his shoulder during the chant and laughed to find his mini version of himself holding up his tiny middle fingers proudly and chanting along with the audience. Many people around the boy held up their beers and smiled big at the little guy, who basked joyfully in the approval of the crowd around him.

The guys were already starting the feedback on their guitars. I was standing off on the side of the stage, feeling like I always did before we started our set: like I was going to puke. As I stepped out into the spotlight, the crowd started yelling. They were always a little surprised to see a girl lead singer at a rock show. Some booed right away, some whistled and cheered. On cue, a loud-mouthed dude in the back yelled at me, over the audience, "Take off yer shirt!"

The blonde in the front seized her opportunity, climbed up on the guardrail, turned to the audience, and answered the drunk dude's request. Then she turned to our sixteen-year-old guitar player to share her open secrets with him. For her and his heart's sake, Jared tried his best to keep his eyes

153

on his pedal board. I closed my eyes and prayed for God to seize my voice and sing his love and truth over all of them.

"I will break . . . into your thoughts . . . with what's written on my heart."

Then I screamed with all my heart about wanting to break off every chain of death that held people's hearts captive to addictions, hatred, violence, greed, depression, suicide, self-hate, and on and on.

On this very typical show night, I was, as I always am when I stand on stage, overtaken with the deepest love for this group of people. They were strangers to me, but God had known them all since he formed them in their mother's bellies. It was God's love for them that poured out of my gut as I sang. There was no other reason for me to love them with such aching desperation. I wanted to hug them all at once, so I prayed for God to do what I couldn't.

At one point I saw the blonde girl start to cry. I knew she'd never felt love like this. I knew God was speaking to her and I was praying she would respond and believe that she was more valuable than she had ever understood before.

After the show was over, I was standing beside the merchandise booth where we sold our music and T-shirts, and I saw her. She was stunning up close. Her eyes were a beautiful translucent aqua color I've never seen anywhere else. They sparkled as she talked to me.

"There was something so different about y'all's band. I just loved it," she said through a welcoming smile.

"I was praying for you," I said. "I prayed for God to speak to your heart while we played." I was overwhelmed with love and joy as I spoke to her.

Her face twisted to a look of disgust. "God?" She cussed. "Are you religious?" Now she was rolling her eyes and mocking me.

"No," I said, lowering my head. "I wouldn't consider my-self religious."

"Well, that's good. I didn't come here to get preached at."

Then she pulled down her top and asked me to sign her chest.

"We don't sign chests. I'm sorry. But I'll sign your arm," I said, and went to sign her arm. She quickly pulled her arm away. She cussed me again.

"No, forget you, with yer old holier-than-thou crap," she said as she walked off, hating me.

I loved her so much. She reminded me of me. We didn't share everything in common, but her hatred for Christians sounded like the way I used to hate them.

It wasn't time to talk to our audience about God yet. I should have paid attention to what time it was for her and just showed her love and acceptance, even though she may still have been mad about our "not signing boobs" policy. But this was a good example of what Fly-leaf could do and what it couldn't. We were not gospel preachers. We weren't trying to save souls; God had only put it in us to save lives for now. Later I heard stories of many people coming to faith in Christ during our set at a secular show, even though we had said nothing about God. It was clear that it was not time for us to talk about God. We could only pray that the Spirit would speak for himself as we played.

We could only pray that the Spirit would speak for himself as we played.

And then we could pray that God would send others into the lives of these people who would continue to love them and show them that they were made for more than trying to satisfy their insatiable flesh and blood.

But I knew that if God ever showed me it was time for me to speak, I would. I'd be dead if it wasn't for God pulling me out of my old life. So I was willing to shut up and sing in a dark club full of dying people, just as much as I was willing to tell my story about him whenever he called me to. Ever since I woke up the day after I almost took my own life, I knew my life was no longer my own. It belonged to the God who saved me.

A Restless, Thirsty Spirit

For ten years we continued to play concerts for stadiums full of thirsty people—people who had accepted that their main purpose in life was to spend their lives trying to nurse their flesh (that is never satisfied), just like I did.

We think we're not thirsty when we are drinking.

We think we're satisfied when we get applause.

We think we've arrived when we are making out and feel in love with someone, or when we find something resembling "joy" and laughter when we are high.

We feel purpose as we fight with our lovers for justice and understanding, or when we fight with the girl who needs a slap in the face.

We feel purpose and justice in our violence.

We think we're liberating our children from the weights of society by teaching them to "tell it like it is" and to be just like our restless selves.

We think one day we will retire from work so we can finally rest in this place of recreation and entertainment.

We think, *If we could only listen to music and go to concerts, beaches, and on mountain vacations, and have holidays, then we would be at peace and rest.*

We think our restlessness would be stilled and we'd find satisfaction.

All these things touched the flesh of our audience, as it had touched me my whole life—they feel *alive* and *real* and *almost full.*

And then Flyleaf hits the stage. I can sense the crowd feeling as I had for so long; I can feel them begin to ache inside. The feedback churns and hearts soar. But for what? And then I begin to sing. All at once I'm singing from a vast place of love and adoration for God and I'm speaking into hearts longing for more. Those hearts belong to people . . .

They feel enchanted.

They sense a roar from their own spirit rising up as I scream love and hope.

What was that? Was that my spirit? I have one of those in me? I thought I was full . . .

But then, their epiphany.

Wait, I'm hungry. *I crave. And I've been drinking like a fish yet I'm still thirsty. Is there more to me than flesh and bones? What is aching in me right now?*

We play and scream our hearts out. The audience feels their spirits quake; their hearts are enlightened.

We've opened a door inside of them. It leads to the spirit world by way of God worship—through a sound system, through prayers calling him to descend on our praises.

They feel it. The prayers, the worship, the wind blowing through their spirit doorway. They just don't know what to call it.

They realize that the physical things that bothered them before are small compared to this spiritual plane they are standing on during our concert.

They meet us in a spiritual place when we play. We show them, "You are not really satisfied with the flesh. You are thirsty for the spirit. And that is what we are leading you to: a well of living water to satisfy your spirit."

They respond: "Yes, we *are* thirsty. None of this stuff is satisfying me."

We play our last chord.

We walk off the stage.

We have said nothing about God.

We have only prayed the people in the audience won't die.

We leave them aware of their thirst, saying they are thirsty.

We abandon them in an ocean, praying they don't dehydrate themselves to death drinking the salt water they see in every direction. Sometimes they hate us for not being good enough gods to be God for them afterward. But we aren't omnipresent and we can't stay.

16

I Couldn't Sleep

I was newly married to Josh Sturm and touring to support our album *Memento Mori*. We walked into our room at the Holiday Inn Express and dropped our bags by the door. Josh pulled out his toiletry bag and took it with him to the shower. I pulled out a book someone had loaned me and started at the beginning. It was *23 Minutes in Hell*.

I was suspicious of any book where the author claimed to have gone to heaven or hell and returned to tell the tale. So the whole first part of the book I thought, *Yeah, right*. But then I started to recognize the story. I had heard it before.

Hell Is a Metaphor?

Eight years ago my friend Chad had stopped into town for a visit. I hadn't seen him in a long while. A group of us were hanging out with him when the conversation turned to the topic of hell. People were throwing out hell philosophies left and right. The dialogue escalated until everyone gave up on the discussion except Chad and me. We went through Bible verses we remembered that supported the idea of universalism—the idea that if God loves everyone, and Jesus died for everyone, then in the end everyone will be saved.

"Every knee will bow and every tongue confess that Jesus Christ is Lord."

"It is not God's will that any would perish, but that all would come to repentance through the knowledge of Jesus Christ."

"And didn't Jesus pray to God, 'Thy will be done'? If it isn't God's will that any would perish, then maybe none will. Jesus died for the sins of the whole world, forever. He forgave men when they weren't sorry, as he hung on the cross bleeding, saying what seems to be about his murderers, 'Father, forgive them, for they know not what they do.'"

"So what about all those who don't know?"

Round and round we went, until we concluded that hell was most likely metaphorical.

To Hell and Back

The very next week Flyleaf met for practice. We started with a Bible study like we always did. This time Jared's mom had given us a tape to listen to. It was a speaker named Bill.

The man's voice was quiet, shy, and unimpressive. It was a voice you'd never notice—totally forgettable. I imagined him to be a simple, small-framed, unassuming, unimpressive sort of nerdy guy. In the beginning of the tape I wondered what on earth this guy had to say that was worth a recording of his speech.

But as he got into the story I realized something heart shattering.

This guy had been to hell *and* back. Literally. He told how he woke up in hell with no knowledge of having ever been a Christian. He experienced a period of time *outside* of time, literally an eternity, where he was in hell.

I wanted so much to not believe him, but everything in me knew he was naturally a terrible liar. My heart shook with conflict. I wanted to pass him off as crazy or as a liar, but he showed no hint of either lunacy or dishonesty. I sat there wrecked by what I was hearing, searching for anything in his speech to validate my cynicism. Then he concluded his story, at which point his voice shook.

"I saw Jesus standing there," Bill said, voice quavering, "and I was so relieved and amazed, but also wondering, and my heart asked, 'Why would you bring me here?'

'Because there are many who believe this place does not exist,' he said. 'Even many of my own people don't believe that it's here. I am calling you to tell them.'

In my heart I responded, 'What if they don't believe me? What if they say I just had a nightmare?' And Jesus said so clearly to me, 'It is not your job to convince them; it is only your job to tell them.'"[1]

At that moment, I felt two arrows enter my heart. One exposed me as one of those who loved Jesus and yet twisted the Scriptures to try to prove that hell did not exist. And the other was revelation about the motives of this man. Bill didn't want attention, nor did he possess an agenda for giving this speech. I believed he was genuine. He just wanted to tell his story because Jesus told him to do so.

1. To hear Bill's whole testimony, see "23 Minutes in Hell—Bill Wiese Hell Testimony (Extended Hell Version)," YouTube video, 1:36:51, posted by FreeCDTracts on May 11, 2013, https://www.youtube.com/watch?v=nmrTfyM-hbY. Quotes here can be found at approx. 42:40–44:00.

I then understood God's directive on my heart: he called me to do what Bill was doing as well. He didn't want me to change people's minds about him, just to tell them what he did for me. Bill's story helped me understand that God wanted to use my story to help others as well.

It was a profound moment of conviction, and just like I began to see myself and others in this world so differently after I found Jesus, I also began to see the world in light of eternity much differently after that day.

I remember crying for three days straight after that.

I sat in traffic trying to quit crying so that I could take care of some errands. But when I looked to my left I saw people who may die any second and end up in hell. When I looked to my right I saw the same. I knew Jesus paid the penalty for sin and offered forgiveness. And I knew if only we would believe it, we could receive that forgiveness and be with God when we died. But a life without Jesus translated into an eternity apart from him, an eternity in hell. I wept for what seemed a week over the destiny of the human race without Christ.

> I was weeping for the whole world and no one understood why.

After three days the weight lifted at least somewhat, and I was able to stop crying enough to go about my day until another wave hit. I remember trying to explain my overwhelmed spirit in band practice, but the guys just looked at me like I was insane. I don't think I ever felt more alone. I was weeping for the whole world and no one understood why.

The Weight of Darkness

Fast-forward eight years and there I was, sitting in the hotel room reading this book a friend had given me. I was cynical about the book, waiting for the author to trip up in his story and expose himself as a fake, when all of a sudden I recognized the story. The whole speech I had heard in that band Bible study eight years ago flooded my mind. I realized that I was reading the book written by the quiet awkward guy from that tape.

I started to read more slowly.

My tired husband crawled in bed beside me. He turned off his light and left me reading with my own lamp on low. By the end of the book the tears started. I saw crowds of hundreds of thousands of people, people I had sung in front of, my voice loud enough for each one to hear, and all these people were being ushered over a cliff into hell. What had I done? What had I done with my voice? Why hadn't I told them clearly? Didn't I know? Why didn't I say something when I had the chance?

It was 3:00 a.m. by this time, and I was sobbing uncontrollably. Josh woke up and thought someone had died. He was trying to comfort me and figure out what was wrong at the same time. He was completely bewildered at what to do for me. I couldn't stop sobbing enough to tell him for the next thirty minutes, and finally I explained through sobs.

"Josh, I can see them. The crowds I loved and prayed for, the ones I sang to, the whole world that Jesus had died to save from hell, and they were going by the hundreds of thousands into eternity in hell. These precious creations of God were being lost forever and what was I doing, playing shows for entertainment? I *have* to tell them. I *have* to tell them while they're still listening."

I kept sobbing and sobbing. Finally, after listening and letting me cry for another hour, Josh said sternly, "I don't think you should read that book anymore."

I was so angry. "That is your response? This isn't about a book. This is about something that is really happening every day!"

Josh was overwhelmed, and I think I went to bed weeping. He held me while I cried myself to sleep. What else could he do?

A month later we visited our pastor, Eric, and his wife, Sarah, in Kansas City. They had joined a church and wanted us to meet the guy who started it. His name was Tim Johns. He hugged us like we were his long-lost children. He showed us to the humble living room, where Josh and I sat on an old couch.

When Tim started asking us what we did for a living, Eric started to explain Flyleaf and our mission. Tim asked if we had any music to hear online. So Eric went with him to his computer in the other room and showed him about twenty-five seconds of the "I'm So Sick" video. He was so excited about what he heard that he started yelling to Josh and me about how awesome it was. He returned to the room where Josh and I were sitting and began to explain my whole life to me.

"Lacey! You have a prophetic, evangelical anointing. This is a very heavy, heavy calling. God has poured his love for this generation into your heart and allowed you to sing their song with his heart of passion, so they will know that God loves them. You are called to carry a very heavy burden, but Josh, it is your job to help her take that burden to Jesus and leave it at his feet. You have to remind her constantly that she is not Jesus and that it is not her job to save people, because she can't. She will feel the burden so that she can write and sing the songs from the heart of the Father."

Josh and I just sat there and listened, blown away.

"Lacey, this burden is important in order for you to do what you do, but you cannot live in that place or you will be completely crushed under the weight of it. God has called you to his peace and joy as well, and Josh, it is your job to pull her out of that place of mourning and burden and prayer and take her to the movies, or for a walk, or whatever. This will be hard for her because she will feel like she is wasting time she could be using to save people or help them, but Lacey, you have to let Josh lead you into these places of rest or you will be overwhelmed and no good to anyone. God wants you to learn to listen to Josh and trust that he hears the heart of the Father too. He wants you to rest in knowing that when you trust your husband you will be in the right place at the right time. He will teach you it is not necessary to offend everyone all the time, which you probably do, is that right?"

Josh and I were both crying and had no idea how to respond.

"Yes, that happens a lot," I said, stunned.

"Well, Josh is going to be able to help you know how to get the 'what' done without hurting everyone in your path."

Through his tears, Josh then told Tim about what had happened in the hotel room the other night. "She would not stop sobbing and I didn't know what was going on. I was like, 'Is she really feeling the burden for all these people going to hell, or do I need to cast a demon out so it will stop tormenting her?'"

Tim laughed, and said, "She *really* feels that burden." I was so relieved to hear that. "But Lacey, you have to let him help you take your burdens to Jesus's feet, so you don't try to carry them on your own shoulders. It's too much, sweetheart. And lighten up on your bandmates. They don't carry the burden like you do, and if God sees fit to let them off the hook, then you shouldn't try to put them on it."

Yes, sir. This godly man spoke truth and wisdom into my life—a heavenly message that accomplished much in my heart, lightening my spirit. Oh, my, what freedom! What a weight now falling off my back. I was amazed.

17

The Reason
I Stepped Down
from Flyleaf

*O*hmygodohmygodohmygodohmygod!" I yelled as I ran
from the bathroom, across our bed, stopping just before the hallway where Josh stood looking at me with big eyes.

"What?!"

"Ohmygodohmygodohmygodohmygod!" I answered,
pointing to the bathroom. He ran to the bathroom and
picked up the pregnancy test to find a very dark plus sign
on its screen.

"What does it mean?" he asked, still not sure.

"I'm pregnant!"

It was Halloween 2008. We went to the hospital that night
to confirm the news. A handsome black doctor dressed as a
cowboy shook our hands to congratulate us. He told us to

come back in about a month. Then we would be ten weeks along and they could make sure everything was normal.

On the Tuesday before Thanksgiving, Josh snapped a picture of my joyful face looking up at him with my belly covered in the magic sonogram jelly.

It was just after that picture was taken that we found out the sad and confusing news. There was no baby heartbeat. The sonogram showed one of two possibilities. I was either miscarrying or I had a rare situation called a molar pregnancy, where a sperm fertilizes an empty egg, the cells freak out, and instead of a baby forming, you develop a rapidly growing cancerous mass. They drew some blood and sent us home to wait for the results.

We sat in shocked silence at home until the phone rang that evening. My doctor's kind, motherly voice let me know that I wasn't miscarrying. She suggested I come in as soon as possible to have a D&C so they could remove the mass growing in my abdomen.

As a believer in miracles, I asked her, "Will it take care of itself if I just leave it alone? Will it dissolve or something?"

"If you do nothing, you will die," she said, very sternly. "It will spread to your lungs very quickly, then even faster to your brain, and you will die."

"Can I please think about this?"

"I'd like to schedule you for tomorrow morning, if possible," she said.

"Can I wait a couple of days, till after Thanksgiving?"

"You know what, that might be best. With molar pregnancies the chance of hemorrhage during D&C is extremely high. If you wait until after Thanksgiving there will be a better chance of having more blood available in case you need a transfusion. That's fine, but absolutely no later than the morning after Thanksgiving."

You Will Die

Flyleaf had been throwing around titles for the new album for a while, and it was just after this drama played out that Pat suggested the name *Memento Mori*, the Latin phrase that means, "Remember you are mortal and will die." The story goes that in ancient Rome the phrase was used to remind victorious soldiers that they were mortal and could die at any time. It was meant to humble the soldiers but also to encourage people to live life to the fullest, because one day you will die and today could be your last.

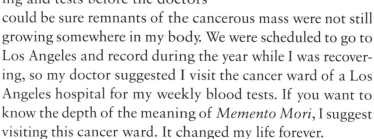

Pat didn't know all that I had just been through with my molar pregnancy when he suggested the name, but it felt prophetic to me after my experience. We all loved it for our own reasons and settled on the name *Memento Mori* for what we didn't know would be the last album that we would play live together.

It took a full year of monitoring and tests before the doctors could be sure remnants of the cancerous mass were not still growing somewhere in my body. We were scheduled to go to Los Angeles and record during the year while I was recovering, so my doctor suggested I visit the cancer ward of a Los Angeles hospital for my weekly blood tests. If you want to know the depth of the meaning of *Memento Mori*, I suggest visiting this cancer ward. It changed my life forever.

When Josh and I walked through the doors of the hospital, I was greeted by two people who looked at me with a kind of concern I'd never seen from strangers in Los Angeles. They smiled warmly and lovingly, looked me over, and offered me a refreshment.

"No, thank you," I answered, blushing at their unexpected kindness.

I stepped into the elevator at the same time as another woman, who reached the buttons before me.

"What floor are you going to?" she asked,

"Oh, looks like the same as you," I answered.

The woman began to search my eyes with loving, hopeful concern as the doors closed.

"This is a wonderful place to be. I just want to tell you that."

Kindness and hope dripped from her voice as she went on with the kind of intimate tone that she would use with a sister or a daughter who was afraid.

"They certainly keep you alive here."

Her smile broadened into a look of an overcomer who was proud to have a moment to breathe and speak encouragement to a young person like me facing the prospect of cancer.

I smiled back at her as my eyes filled up with tears and told her thank you, squeezing Josh's hand extra tight.

I kept thinking, *She is so brave and selfless to try to encourage me this way. I'm a stranger to her, but she is looking at me like an old friend. She has been through so much, and yet she is the one encouraging me.*

I felt ashamed at how few times in my life I had treated a stranger with the kind of love this woman was showing me. She said so much with just a few words and her body language. I was humbled by her love. But my lessons on how to love a stranger who could die any day were just beginning.

I stepped off the elevator and walked into a room that seemed to smile with warmth. Fresh flowers and a colorful fish tank accented the room, while the smell of freshly baked cookies stirred a desire in me to curl up and take a nap. Glowing, beautiful, friendly faces dotted the room. They all seemed to zone in on me one at a time. Whenever my eyes would meet any of theirs, they looked welcoming and encouraging.

I walked to the check-in window. The woman behind the desk looked at me with a joy so sweet and humble that I wondered if she was an angel in disguise.

"What a beautiful face!" she said to me.

The sincerity of her compliment was surprising. She didn't wait for a response. "My love, I have some papers for you."

"Thank you," I said as she handed me a clipboard with a little golden Hershey's dark chocolate clipped on top of the papers.

I marveled—this very candy was my absolute favorite. She smiled wide and beautiful at me while looking over the top of her reading glasses and then gave me a suspicious wink, like she knew that chocolate was my favorite kind. I went back to my seat, grabbed Josh's hand, and whispered in his ear, "I think that lady is an angel, for real."

Before I could start filling out my papers another lady in the waiting room brought me a cookie in a napkin.

"Hello, sweet one! My friend Elise baked these cookies for the waiting room today, and I just brought them over. They are still slightly warm and nice and soft, if you want to try one."

"Oh, thank you," I answered, taking the cookie even though I didn't really want it. I didn't want to take away her joy at being able to be generous and hospitable. She made me feel *so* loved. She was so happy that I received her gift.

I began to fill out the form again, but I didn't get far before another woman came over and knelt down in front of me.

She took both my hands in hers. "What is your name, darling?"

"Lacey."

"Lacey! That is beautiful."

171

She lowered her voice to almost a whisper. "May I ask what area of your body you're having issues in?"

The woman was older and seemed like a concerned grandmother.

"Um . . . my uh . . . abdomen." I was unsure of what she really wanted to know.

"I had a feeling that might have been so. Let me tell you, Lacey, I had issues in the same area. I want to tell you that I am totally better now! I'm only here for check-ups. I want you to know, Lacey, that you are going to be okay."

"Thank you," I said as she squeezed my hands and kissed them before walking back to her seat.

I just got started on my form again when another older Hispanic woman came and stood in front of me. She just looked at me for a moment. With tears in her eyes she smiled warmly at me but said nothing.

"Hello," I said to her.

She answered me in Spanish.

"I'm sorry, I don't speak Spanish," I said.

"No?" she answered, with a thick accent. "You look like my daughter." She smiled, making a tear fall from her eye.

She leaned down, took my face in her hands, and looked at me with such love I almost started bawling. Then she kissed me on each cheek and gave me a long, genuine, loving hug. I would guess she was praying as she hugged me. It was as if she really believed her hug was going to heal me.

"You will be okay," she said to me.

I was wiping tears from my eyes now, overwhelmed with how loved I felt in the waiting room of this cancer center.

I sat there utterly convicted.

I realized I had only a nice concept in my mind when I spouted off speeches at Flyleaf shows about how we should love people because we never know if it will be our last day or theirs. I had no idea what that really looked like until I sat in that waiting room. *Memento Mori* came to life in that place, but this was only the beginning.

Life, Our Special Gift

I didn't know at the time that I would survive that process and move on. I didn't know that I would become pregnant with my first child around the same time the next year. I didn't know that I would go to a very painful, unexpected funeral the year after that. I didn't know that *Memento Mori* would mean so much more to me than I could ever read about or philosophize about.

Memento Mori came to life in tragic ways, with my molar pregnancy and the death of my friend Rich Caldwell, who was killed in a car accident, and it came to life in beautiful, miraculous ways, with the birth of my two sons.

To remember we are mortal means to live one day at a time.

It means we must do the most we can with every day we have. It means we must learn to be truly alive *right now*. We must love people while we can.

To love others doesn't mean we should try to be God for people. If we try to be God for others, we will always let them down and we will always be crushed under the weight of trying to be more than it is possible for us to be. To love others means to point to the God who is our only Savior. It means to look to God to find out where he wants us to go and how he wants us to live and to love. It means we must make the most of every opportunity—that might look like standing on stage in front of thousands and singing your heart out,

> We must learn to be truly alive *right now*. We must love people while we can.

173

or it could be bringing some fresh baked cookies to a cancer ward waiting room. Both are *equally* important. It's just a matter of what your highest purpose is for each day.

We don't know if we will have tomorrow. Sometimes it takes the scary prospect of cancer for that to really sink in. Sometimes it takes a healthy loved one dying in a car crash. Sometimes it takes going through a complicated pregnancy and giving birth to a healthy baby anyway. But we don't require the experience of trauma to wake up, listen, believe, and truly live like our lives are precious, fragile gifts. The lives of the people around us are precious, fragile gifts.

All life is a gift from God.

> Don't neglect what you know you should do with the short time you have here on earth.

So if you know you should leave home and tell the world about hope by being a musician, lawyer, doctor, missionary, businessperson, educator, or whatever; or if you are supposed to go home and be a mom, a son, a friend, or a plumber at your dad's plumbing business, then don't neglect what you know you should do with the short time you have here on earth.

For me, the season for being in Flyleaf was coming to a close, and I could feel it. When my son Jack was born, I wasn't certain how having a baby would affect me as a full-time musician, but I knew my priorities were already changing.

I remember lying beside my baby boy, looking at his innocent face, and wishing that my only job was to be his momma. But I wasn't sure this was what I was meant to do. I remember crying and praying and telling the Lord, "I'm willing to trust you, if you want me to hire help and keep touring. But if you honor me by calling me to stay home, then I will be so happy."

It took a full year of praying and watching for the answer before Josh and I would make one of the hardest decisions we've ever had to make. But finally, the answer was very clear: this new season for us was best served at home, learning what it meant to be parents.

It was hard for a lot of people to understand (especially if they didn't have children) how changing diapers was more important than trying to spread hope into the hearts of suicidal teens through Flyleaf's music. The truth is, it isn't *more* important. It is *just as* important. What matters is knowing what season it is for you and knowing what you are meant to be doing today. That is where you will be the most fulfilled and where you will be the most effective at changing the world.

Voice Less

I had been in Flyleaf for seven years before I ever went to a voice doctor. They stuck a camera down my throat to prove to me that I had destroyed my vocal cords. The first time I saw Dr. Pertzog, we had a show that night in Pittsburgh.

She was shocked.

"You mean to tell me that you are in the middle of a tour?"

"Well," I said, "we are almost done. We only have three more dates."

"And you are supposed to play tonight?"

"Yeah, at Mr. Smalls Theatre," I rasped.

"You think you are going to sing for an hour tonight?"

"Well, our set is around an hour, yeah."

"Listen. I know you are saying that you have these shows booked, but I'm going to strongly recommend that you do not sing at all. Not at all. I have no idea how you have any voice left, but if you do not stop right now, you will lose your voice completely."

"You mean I won't be able to finish the tour?"

"I mean you won't have a voice to sing your children to sleep with."

My heart sank.

"At this point, you are going to have to stay completely silent for a good three months. The only other alternative is surgery. With surgery you risk losing your voice or at least dramatically changing it. My recommendation is that you go on voice rest."

"So can I at least finish these last few shows?"

"Absolutely not."

After three months of vocal rest and some therapy, my voice was closer to being normal, but it has never been the same.

Toward the end, my voice was one of the most stressful things about touring. I never knew if it would work or not. My only peace, besides praying and being sure I was supposed to be singing, was knowing that Rich was behind the soundboard. He knew me so well. After ten years of playing live shows together, he could tell when my voice was tired. He knew exactly which parts I struggled with. He knew just when I needed effects, or to be buried or pulled up in the mix. He knew the songs so well. Most of all, he knew my voice and understood how it worked better than I did.

He took the blame when my voice was shot. He would turn up the guitars so no one could hear that I sounded like a dying horse. He didn't care if anyone commented on the mix being bad because they couldn't hear the vocals. He had my back and always knew just how to cover for me. Because of this, many times Rich was the only reason the show could go on. I never thought I would have to play a show without Rich—he was the author of the Flyleaf live show sound. In many ways, Rich was the person who gave me a voice to tour with.

The last time I saw Dr. Pertzog, we were finishing up what would turn out to be my last Flyleaf tour. I was five months pregnant and my voice was acting up again. She explained how pregnancy hormones affect the voice. Sometimes the effects are permanent, but most of the time they go away after nursing stops. She explained how I had lost some of my range, and she didn't know if those notes would come back or not until my baby was born—maybe not until after I finished nursing.

Rich Less

Rich had taught our monitor engineer, Shawn, everything he could teach him about running the front of house sound-board. So Shawn was as close as we could get to Rich being behind the board. And tonight, Shawn was out there. But even though Shawn was good, he didn't know my voice like Rich.

Shawn would have been fine on a good night, but this was not a good night. This night would be the most difficult show I would ever have to play. My thoughts overwhelmed me.

I can't do this. I can't do this. It's just not right. Nothing is right anymore. I can't do this.

I could barely breathe.

There was a room full of people out there waiting for us. They had all bought a ticket to the show so we could raise money for our tour manager, Katy, and her two-year-old son, Kirby. Katy was Rich's wife—and now his widow.

Katy and Kirby's lives would never be the same without Rich.

We were all aching deeply as we mourned with them.

Rich had given his whole life to Flyleaf. He had quit his big-money job—the one he went to college for—where he sat in a cubicle. He knew something was missing, like so many people do when they settle for less than the heights to which they're called. But Rich knew how to live his life to the fullest: *by faith*.

Faith involves risk. Rich took a risk so he could pile into a 1988 Ford Club Wagon van with five kids and their instruments and tour the country with no guarantees. He believed in us. And more than believing in us, he believed in the impact and difference we could make. That was ten years ago, now. Over a million albums sold, many world tours, and thousands of letters from fans talking about how Flyleaf music saved their lives.

It turns out Rich made the right choice. Maybe it was Rich's faith that brought us so far. He was definitely a place of creativity, peace, laughter, and perspective we all needed during those years.

Once we had the opportunity to travel to Afghanistan to play for the troops. Rich mentioned to me that his mother was terrified of him going into a war zone. He said, "Mom, all I can do in this life is go and do whatever God wants me to do." He felt like God really wanted him to go. "If I'm supposed to die in Afghanistan," he said to his mom, "then at least I can find comfort knowing that Afghanistan is where God wanted me to die."

I think about what Rich said about this almost daily. So many men and women serving over there have left their families and carry such an emotional weight, risking their lives and missing their loved ones. We were honored to be invited to play for them and serve them in this small way. We spent a week there, traveling from base to base.

One day they told us that the base we had visited the day before had been attacked and several men had died. I wept, wondering if I had said what God wanted me to say—if I had said what I *should* have said. That night we were all exhausted because of little sleep and bad jet lag. But there were two soldiers we talked to earlier who were asking Rich questions about God. When I went to bed Rich and the soldiers were still sitting in the back of an ATV, talking.

The next morning I awoke as the sun was rising. When I walked out of my cabin, Rich was still there with those guys, watching the sunrise and talking about God.

"You never know if today is going to be your last, or their last. *Memento mori*, right?" he had said to me when I marveled at his sleepless night. His commitment to our message was humbling. He was living it out and challenging me with his love for others. He did this at our shows as well. While everyone was stressed and complaining, Rich worked to keep everyone positive and looking on the bright side.

Rich held so much of Flyleaf together that, on this night, preparing to play without him was too much. We were all a mess.

We hardly had any idea what to do. This show wasn't going to be the same because Rich was the one who had always made it all happen. That was more apparent now than ever, now that he was missing when we went to load the trailer, load in the venue, set up our gear, and especially now that my voice, so unpredictable, had changed. We all needed him in order to do this well. It was painfully obvious. And we had been mourning about this, and so much more, all day.

I stood on the side stage as the crowd noise boiled into the room. It was time.

James, Pat, and Jared walked up the stairs. My stomach shot up into my throat and I crumpled into a heap. Sameer was behind me. He caught my arm as I went down. I started sobbing.

"I can't do this, I can't do this. I can't, I can't, I can't."

Sameer wrapped me up in his arms and started sobbing with me. His sobs were deep and loud. We let ourselves fall apart a little more than we had all day in that moment.

"I love you, Sameer," I said as I cried.

"I love you too," he cried.

"I'm so sorry that I haven't appreciated you like I should. I don't feel like I've appreciated anyone like I should, especially Rich," I said, still sobbing. "I don't know how to do this without him."

We just held each other. He squeezed me so tight. It was the way you squeeze someone when you're not sure if you'll ever see them again. That was our message, wasn't it? *Memento mori.* Love like it may be your loved one's last day. Hadn't all this painted that message in living color? Weren't we living out *memento mori* as we mourned our brother Rich and as we apologized to and loved on each other? What else could we do?

"I love you, Lacey," Sameer said again.

"I love you too," I repeated. "Thank you, Sameer."

I meant it with everything in me. I was so thankful for my brother in that moment. I needed to hold someone and be held by someone who had been a part of our Flyleaf family—someone who understood why everything felt wrong about going on with our show without Rich.

Thank you for that moment, Sameer. I will never forget it. We pulled away, wiped our faces, and put in our earbuds as we walked on stage.

Turning Leaves

The show wasn't anything close to normal. There was a sweet encouragement and kindness between us all on stage. There was sensitivity among us with this being the first show after Rich's death. My voice worked and then it wouldn't. My memory worked and then it wouldn't. My heart broke over and over until the last note played and I exhaled.

> I have to learn from the way Rich lived his life so fully, with faith and risk.

The show was harder than any other show I'd ever played. It was obvious to me that this was the most beautiful and saddest part of the winter. It was a season ending. Flyleaf would never be the same.

I knew that my time in Flyleaf was over. I mourned so many things that night.

I'm jealous of Rich for making it to heaven before me. I know he would tease me about it if I could talk to him.

"Haha! I know more about this place than you!" he'd say.

And although I can't wait for Rich to show me around, I have to wait, because I am still breathing. I have to learn from the way Rich lived his life so fully, with faith and risk.

I must always remember that I will die, and I must remember this so that I can remember to *live*. Heaven is Rich's new horizon, and until we get there we all have our own new horizons here on earth to explore.

Memento mori.

Memento vivere.

18

THE REASON
God Will Always Love Us

I call my son Jack the Brave. I believe he has a gift of bravery even though the little guy seems to have been afraid of almost everything since he was born. The more I tell him he is brave, the braver I watch him become. He will say, "I scared, Momma" as we walk past a weird-looking mannequin in a store. I respond, "No, Jack isn't scared. He is brave." He will peek out from behind my legs where he is trying to hide and say, "I bave." Then he will stare the thing down with courage, even though he is still really, really nervous about it. That's when I just want to cheer for him. He always looks at me in those moments, to make sure that my face is telling him, "It's all going to be okay." It helps him tremendously to know I am not scared of the weird-looking, frozen, plastic person.

Sometimes Jack the Brave has bad days. With meltdown after meltdown he will hit and kick and throw things, trying to break stuff in his frustration. He will scream and cry, cry, cry. The easy thing would be to do whatever I can to just make him happy, so he will stop crying, stop having fits, stop throwing things. The easy thing would be for me to tiptoe around him, doing whatever I can to appease him and avoid a breakdown. It would be easier for me to stick him in a room by himself so he can destroy whatever he wants and have his rampaging way all alone. It would be easier to distract him and change the subject, ignoring the tantrum so neither he nor I will have to deal with his "issues."

But I don't believe any of these things represent the loving thing to do.

Listen, I'm not trying to give parenting advice. I've only been a mom for two and a half years. I have taken no classes and read very little on the subject. I'm just being vulnerable with you right now and talking about what goes on in my heart while trying to love my son. I care about Jack the Brave's heart. I want to train his heart to be kind, loving, generous, self-controlled, patient, hopeful, and full of faith. I realize that these things must be in me in order for him to really get it. If I throw my grown-up version of a tantrum, I can't be too shocked when I see him throw his two-year-old version. If I am always complaining, I can't be surprised when he whines. So when I'm praying for Jack and trying to discipline his heart to develop good character, I pray for myself and work to discipline my own heart as well.

But disciplining a strong-willed two-year-old who is just as passionate as I am is hard work. Sometimes he consumes my focus for an entire day. Sometimes I feel like I have disciplined all day long. The whole day I search for ways to encourage Jack for the slightest sign of anything praiseworthy. I tell him, "If you obey Mommy, and follow directions, if you stop pitching fits and whining, then we can have so much fun today." I watch for moments of fun and seize them whenever they surface.

But some days we hardly have any fun. Sometimes he falls asleep in my arms, crying, saying, "Oh, Momma, I sawy. I sawy, Momma."

"I forgive you, Jack," I say. "I love you. Momma always loves you, Jack. I'm so proud of you. You are so brave. You are such a good boy."

Finally, when he relaxes in my arms, and his breathing becomes slow and heavy, I lay him in his bed. When I look down at his sleeping face I am overwhelmed with love. He is my son. Even though we had a bad day, he possesses my heart—I love him with a crazy and deep love. I thank God it wasn't the kind of bad day we used to have whenever he struggled with asthma as an infant. Those bad days were of a different sort: staying in the hospital with breathing treatments, IVs, and pneumonia, over and over. I'm thankful for Jack no matter what kind of day we have together: a bad day at a hospital, a bad day at home, or one of the many wonderful days we have. I love him so much.

You Are the Reason

My encounters with God have taught me how extravagant and high his love soars above earthly love. His love is infinitely greater in capacity, patience, and perfection. Even so, being a mom helps me to understand God's love for me in a much deeper way. After a long day of discipline, meltdowns, disobedience, and fits, I look at my sleeping boy and love him so *completely*. My hope for him is so full and beautiful.

The Bible says that to God a day is like a thousand years, and a thousand years is like a day. I believe even after we spend a lifetime sinning and being deceived, confused, angry, heartbroken, and hateful, and after we have made a reckless mess of our lives, God looks at us with love. He has an even deeper love, patience, and hope for us, his creation, than any mom could ever have for her child. His love is so much better than ours. His love for us is perfect. There is no one outside of that love. There is no one God would reject, only those who might reject him.

A girl named Taylor wrote me an email a few years ago. She sounded so much like myself at her age. She was depressed, confused, cutting, and suicidal. She said that Flyleaf's music had helped her through, but she still struggled. I had never met her before, but as I read her email, I was overwhelmed with love for her. I love her because the God I love created her. It was obvious she had no idea how valuable she was. She didn't understand the perfect love God has for her. I wrote her a letter in response to her email to tell her God loves her and has a great plan for her life.

Taylor wanted me to share what I wrote with you, because much of what I said to her I also want to say to you.

Hi Taylor!

Are you fourteen? You sound a lot older. Thank you for your message. I'm sorry I missed it earlier. It never gets old hearing the way God does miracles in people's lives. We prayed our music would speak his healing, freedom, and deliverance to people—salvation only God can bring to people.

You remind me of myself when I was your age in a lot of ways. I'm so glad God spoke to your heart when you heard my story. He loves you and has a plan for your life that is so far beyond what you can imagine for yourself. I don't mean fame, or success the way the world thinks of it. But it could be a moment with your firstborn in your arms when you realize he or she wouldn't be alive if God hadn't rescued you, or a moment with a girl whose life was saved because you were brave enough to share your story.

There is a daily purpose for your life that is so important. Some days it is just to learn about God. Sometimes it is to pray for someone and move mountains with your faith. Some days it is to say "Hi" to someone who needs to know they aren't invisible. Your very breath moves the air and as long as it does that, you are changing the world.

I pray you would not settle for less than fulfilling God's highest purpose for your life in every way. I pray you would know what it means to have wisdom, love, and the power of God, to bring healing, freedom, and truth to everyone you come in contact with. Even if it's just by your presence, carrying God's Spirit with you and changing the atmosphere by just being there.

I pray you would heal from all the injustices that happened in your life. I pray you would fight for justice for others and help bring victory to them. I pray you would know how the enemy of your soul fears your faith in God. The enemy knows how your faith will rip people out of his hands of death and place them into Christ's hands of life. He knows God made you and that you reflect the character and beauty of God. He knows if you trust Jesus and follow him as Lord, you will be one of the ones who will judge angels in eternity, and cast demons out by the power of Jesus's name on earth.

You are a powerful work of God's art, Taylor. You have no idea the amazing plans God has for your life.

Don't settle for cheap imitations. Not in romance, not in art, not in influence. Don't settle, just because you can't imagine how much greater and fuller you could be if you would trust God with your life. I'm only a girl who said yes to God. No different than you, except that I put my trust in him and have given him all that I was and am every day. Today I try to give him all that I am, and trust him. Because of that, I am choosing not to limit my life and my gifts to my own generic plans for myself.

God made us so he could love us. We will feel restless and empty, and always come up short, if we try to find purpose anywhere else.

God is so kind, Taylor. His love is the only true love. That's why every other imitation of it leaves us empty. That's why our hearts burn within us every time we hear someone tell us with sincerity, "God loves you." God made us so he could love us. We will feel restless and empty, and always come up short, if we try to find purpose anywhere else.

Thank you for listening to our music. Thank you for paying attention to the lyrics. I pray God gives you the words to help people understand the love and wisdom of God in ways they never did before, through your poems. I pray you would use your gift of words for God's glory and that they would save people from death, physically, emotionally, and spiritually. Amen!

God has given Taylor a gift of words. She uses her words to tell stories and write poems that make people feel deeply. She had used this gift to write many sad, hopeless poems. I encouraged her to not settle for limiting her gift in a way that will only bring her glory. I encouraged her to use her gift to

188

bring glory to God. So she wrote a poem that still brings me life when I read it.

> We make empty wishes upon stars that have already
>   begun to burn away,
> We add false color to hair that has already begun to
>   grey.
> We place lively spring flowers at the feet of the dead,
> And we only voice our most meaningful words on
>   our deathbeds.
> Why is it that we try so hard to paint colors onto
>   things that have already faded away,
> Yet we never open our eyes to see the bright hues of
>   today?

When I open my eyes to the bright hues of today, I think of you. I want you to know you are beautiful. I want you to see the beauty of life around you. I want you to fulfill the highest heights for which you were created.

Do you realize God created you? You are his idea, a reflection of God's glory.

The God I love created you. While I still have today on this earth to love, I want to love you, dear reader. I want you to know that no matter who you are, no matter what you believe, no matter what you do or what you have done, God loves you.

I am alive because God loves me and sent his only begotten Son, Jesus Christ, to die on a cross for my sins.

I am alive, and Christ is The Reason.

God loved the world so much that he gave his only begotten Son, so that whoever believes in him should not perish, but have everlasting life—life to the *full*. Christ died so you could live, because he loves you.

You are The Reason.

You and I were made to be lovers of God. There is no other love greater. There is nothing else that will give us more life.

Your Tomorrow

*Y*ou and I are traveling on different paths. Though we may share similar experiences and enjoy the same things, each of us is unique. My journey took many turns and dips and crashes. But each bend in the road of life—each dip and crash—adds a little bit more beauty to us as people. Those experiences and scars left by themselves will certainly fester and turn an ugly color, turning us ugly. But God took my experiences and crashes and turned them into something surprising, something magnificent: *joy*.

God made you for a purpose. It is important and beautiful. Your life is a gift to you and to the world around you. We settle for so much less than we are created for when we give our lives to money, work, pride, drugs, abuse, suicide, dreams, family, friends, and lovers. God made us to be his alone.

C. S. Lewis wrote:

> Our Lord finds our desires not too strong, but too weak. We are half-hearted creatures, fooling about with drink and sex and ambition when infinite joy is offered us, like an ignorant child who wants to go on making mud pies in a slum because

he cannot imagine what is meant by the offer of a holiday at the sea. We are far too easily pleased.[1]

I love that, and it's so true! I don't want to settle for mud pies. I want to experience God in all his glory. I want his desires to become my desires.

When we give God our lives, we become our truest selves, and we are able to find our greatest purpose and fulfill our highest callings. It's only in God that humanity's restless soul can be satisfied, because humanity was made by God to be his bride. He is the greatest love of our lives. He is our true love. He is all we are ever searching for.

He is the reason we breathe and our only place of true rest and peace. He is our Father, our Creator, our lover, and our best friend. We are alive to be loved by God. He's made us alive by sending his Son Jesus to die for all our sins so that we can be forgiven and made whole again. Jesus rose from the dead and overcame death so that, in Christ, we too will overcome death when we die. After he rose from the dead, Jesus sat down in heaven at the right hand of the Father, where he now intercedes for all of us.

But he didn't leave us orphans. He sent us his Holy Spirit to live in our hearts, every day, all the time, so we would never have to be alone or without him. All we have to do is repent of our sins and give up all that we have settled for that is so much less than we were created for, and he will forgive us. Then, as we invite him to be the Lord of our lives, we will begin to find the fullness of life, peace, joy, hope, and faith that we are made for. We are made to be his alone.

Here's a song I wrote that describes everything I've just told you. I sing it to God often after I share my story. Maybe you could sing it to him too.

1. Lewis, *Weight of Glory*, 26.

The Reason

All my life I searched for something,
To satisfy the longing in my heart
and every time I'd come away emptier than before

And now I finally see *the reason*
It's because I was made to be yours alone

You formed my heart with your own hands
But I just could not understand
That if I gave you my life,
I'd be healed by your grace
I was made for your love
And gave others your place

I spent my days giving my heart away
To anything new
Only to ache from the poison of my
Temporary muse
There were times I'd cry myself to sleep at night
Only to wake up
Wishing that I didn't

And now I finally see *the reason*
'Cause I was made to be yours alone

You formed my heart with your own hands
But I just could not understand
That if I gave you my life
I'd be healed by your grace
I was made for your love
And gave others your place

Thank you for never giving up on me
When I looked to everything else and lived so selfishly
You bled and you died to be with me,
Why would you do something like that for someone
    like me?

Now I finally see *the reason*
Because I was made to be yours alone.

You formed my heart with your own hands
And now I finally understand
And I give you my life
And I'm healed by your grace
I was made for your love that no one can replace
This is it,
I won't miss
Everything I am made for . . .
To be yours
I'm all yours . . .

Now that you know a little about my story, and me, I look forward to talking with you again through another book—I have all kinds of ideas!—and through my blog and through social media. My husband, Josh, and I have also written new music, including songs inspired by this book! Though we're all on unique paths, the beauty of this life is that we can encourage each other, be there for each other in different ways, and love one another through everything.

Afterword

The reason I know Lacey Sturm is simple. She and her band have been guest artists at Rock the River evangelistic meetings—festivals sponsored by the Billy Graham Evangelistic Association (BGEA)—where I preach the gospel of the Lord Jesus Christ to all age groups, but primarily to the youth across America.

The message is powerful. The message is simple. And the message is of vital importance because people everywhere are in desperate need.

God made you, he created you, and he loves you. God wants to heal your heart. He wants you to experience his love and discover his plan and purpose for your life; but the problem Lacey faced, and that we all face, is that we are sinners and sin separates us from God. Yet, "God so loved the world, that he gave his only begotten Son, that whosoever believeth in him should not perish, but have everlasting life" (John 3:16 KJV). Jesus said, "I am the way, the truth, and the life: no man cometh unto the Father, but by me" (14:6 KJV).

Are you willing to turn from your sins and believe on the name of the Lord Jesus Christ? If you are, God will forgive your sins and, like he did for Lacey, he will turn your life around. He gave her a reason for living.

If you would like to experience what Lacey experienced, pray this prayer:

> *Dear God,*
>
> *I am a sinner. I am sorry for my sins. I want to turn from my sins.*
>
> *I believe that Jesus Christ is your Son, that he died for me upon the cross, that he was buried for my sins, and that he was raised to life.*
>
> *I want to trust Jesus now as my Savior and follow him as my Lord from this day forward forevermore.*
>
> *Amen.*

If you have prayed this prayer, write to Lacey. I know that she would like to hear from you. You can visit LaceySturm .com/TheReason to find out how you can connect with someone to talk to and pray with about your decision.

Franklin Graham

Acknowledgments

I've always looked at books with wonder. How do people write so many words, and create worlds with just an alphabet and some paper? It is still very mystical to me. So the first person I have to acknowledge is the God who created humans with language, imagination, and reason. Thank you, God, for our ability to reflect and learn. You wrote the story of life itself and decided to include the tiny thread of my life in the tapestry of your grand masterpiece. Thank you, Jesus, for being the source of life in my heart and turning my worst moments of death into testimonies of life and overcoming.

Thank you to my husband, Joshua, for believing I could write a book before the thought could have ever entered my mind. I would never have attempted this if you hadn't told me I could do it.

Thank you, Mom, for giving me life. Thank you for all the time you spent sharing stories with me. Thank you for your willingness to let a few of the thousands of miracles God has done in our family be written and shared so that other people might be inspired to push through and not give up. You are one of the most phenomenal women I've ever known or heard of. You are beautiful. I love you.

Thank you, Jack and Arrow, for being patient with your momma and loving me so freely. I've never been loved like you boys love me. You are my favorites. I love you forever. I like you for always.

Thank you, Eric, Jazz, Phil, Stevie, and Roman. You are all creative, inspiring, challenging, and brilliant. You have each called passion, freedom, and whimsy out of my heart, making life more beautiful to me, especially during a time when I couldn't see beauty anywhere else.

Thank you, Granny, for being passionate, generous, prayerful, and persistent. I wouldn't be alive without you. Thank you, Gramps, for being the steadiest thing I ever saw growing up. Thank you for not giving up on me when I wanted to give up on myself.

Thank you, Sturm family: Mom, Dad, Jason, Joelene, and Ziggy. I have the greatest in-laws I could ask for. I love this family so much; it brings me to tears thinking of all of you. You have taught me so much in the past six years and I'm honored to be a part of your tree. Thank you for giving Jack and Arrow a loving, fun place to play and learn while I wrote much of this book.

Thank you, Erica Haney, for helping me in the most important areas of my life so I could have the freedom to roam around in my memories and write. God bless you for your willingness to love my kids and me.

Thank you, Tim, Chris, and Pixie Willards. Your patience with the endless rewriting and my overexplaining is something I don't think I've ever seen. You are a beautiful, inspiring family, and the Sturms are thankful to feel like you all are family to us. Tim, your words and wisdom are a signature as unique as your thumbprint. I'm honored to have gotten to work with you on this book. I'm still wondering about how to answer the questions people will have about their favorite quotes "from me," when all their favorite quotes will be something beautiful you wrote!

Thank you, Papa Robb Kelley, for prophesying about this book's existence years before the writing began.

Thank you, Eric and Sarah Patrick, for teaching me so much, and praying for me when I was closest to death. When I was sixteen and you didn't know me, and when I was twenty-six and you knew me better than I knew myself. Both times, your prayers rescued me. Thank you.

Thank you, Flyleaf family, crew, Melanie Savoie, Deb Klein, Octone Records. We did impossible things together. You will always be like my flesh and blood family. Thank you for your years of patience with me. You saw me at my worst and didn't leave me. You're profound in so many ways. Because of my memories of you all, I'm still learning so much from you. And thank you, Kristen May, for helping us all by stepping in, letting me go home, and letting the guys keep going. You're awesome. And your new music is something refreshing and truly a beautiful New Horizon.

Thank you, Matt Yates and Baker Books. You are a team of people who make miraculous things happen. I'm so blessed to know you.

Thank you, J. W., Dina, Jordan, and Walker Clarke. You have been there to help encourage me every step of the way and make sure I know that I'm not crazy. Jordan, your illustrations are beautiful and will speak to millions of people.

Thank you, Franklin Graham and BGEA. You are the biggest encouragement I have to tell my story. You bring so much freedom in my life by letting me know I can be myself. I'm thankful to be one of your millions of spiritual children.

Thank you, Ryan and Crystal Ries, Sonny Sandoval, Brian "Head" Welch, and the Whosoever family. You are doing miraculous things just by being you. You are reaching out to the ones no one else is reaching. You are a glorious, perplexing wonder. Thank you for letting me be a part of what God is doing through you guys.

Thank you to every fan who truly listened and cared enough to want to know what was behind the music. I believe in you all. Thank you to all the ones who heard of us and understood our need for prayers and encouragement. Brittany Wigand, you are so inspiring to me. Thank you to all of you who have written me emails and encouraged me.

About Lacey

*L*acey is a mother, a wife, a rock-and-roll princess, a writer, a speaker, and a solo artist. But most of all, she's a child of God and she desires for others to know and understand how special, how beautiful, how kaleidoscopically wonderful they are made.

Lacey loves Jack and Arrow. Jack is three and Arrow is one, but both boys already have Mommy's passion. Lacey is Josh's wife and loves being a wife. Josh is Lacey's biggest fan, after Jack and Arrow, of course. Their love looks like Play-Doh—it's colorful, makes beautiful things, and expands the more it's tinkered with.

Lacey stands at four feet eleven inches. But she possesses a voice five times that size. Its unmistakable passion, power, beauty, and grit make her impossible to ignore on the airwaves. In 2012 Lacey released her final record with Flyleaf, *New Horizons*. Now she is focused on a new chapter of her life: her family and her new career as an author, speaker, and solo artist.

Lacey continues to do work with the BGEA as well as the Whosoever Movement, an organization she helped found with some of her closest friends from the rock music and extreme sports industries. The Whosoever Movement seeks to build and strengthen at-risk youth in local communities by using their collective passion for music, skateboarding, art, and today's youth culture to creatively inspire people to stand together and work for change.

Connect with Lacey

I'd love to connect with you. Below are several ways we can do that. Check my website for appearances, concerts, book signings, and speaking engagements. Or just drop me a line or shout-out on Twitter.

With love,

Lacey

www.laceysturm.com

Twitter.com/LaceySturm

Facebook.com/LaceySturm81

KEEP IN TOUCH WITH LACEY
and see her upcoming events at:

LACEYSTURM.COM

@LaceySturm

@ilovejoshsturm

LaceySturm81

LaceySturm81